Expecting a Miracle

A Companion Through Pregnancy

Jaymie Stuart Wolfe

BOOKS & MEDIA
Boston

Library of Congress Cataloging-in-Publication Data

Wolfe, Jaymie Stuart.

Expecting a miracle : a companion through pregnancy / by Jaymie Stuart Wolfe.

p. cm.

ISBN 0-8198-2352-X

1. Pregnant women—Prayer-books and devotions—English. 2. Pregnancy—Religious aspects—Christianity. 3. Mothers—Prayer-books and devotions—English. 4. Motherhood—Religious aspects—Christianity. I. Title.

BV4847 .W65 2003
248.8'431—dc21

2003010257

Photos: A. Alvarez—p. 140; Emmanuel Alves, FSP—pp. iv, 14, 36, 76, 154,198; Baehner—pp. 54, 96; FSP Photo Archives—p. 62; Ancilla Christine Hirsch, FSP—pp. 42, 104; James M. Lane—p. 90, 146; Lela T. Lane—132; Thomas W. Lane—p. 20; Kunio Nakajima—p. 70; Madonna Ratliff, FSP—pp. 84, 110, 170, 190; Truong—pp. xii, 124, 162

Printed and published in the U.S.A. by Pauline Books & Media, 50 Saint Pauls Avenue, Boston, MA 02130-3491.

www.pauline.org

Pauline Books & Media is the publishing house of the Daughters of St. Paul, an international congregation of women religious serving the Church with the communications media.

1 2 3 4 5 6 7 8 9 10 10 09 08 07 06 05 04 03

To Mary of Nazareth,
the Loom of the Incarnation,
on whose life was woven
the Light of the World.
May God, our salvation and joy,
weave the image of his holy face
in our hearts.

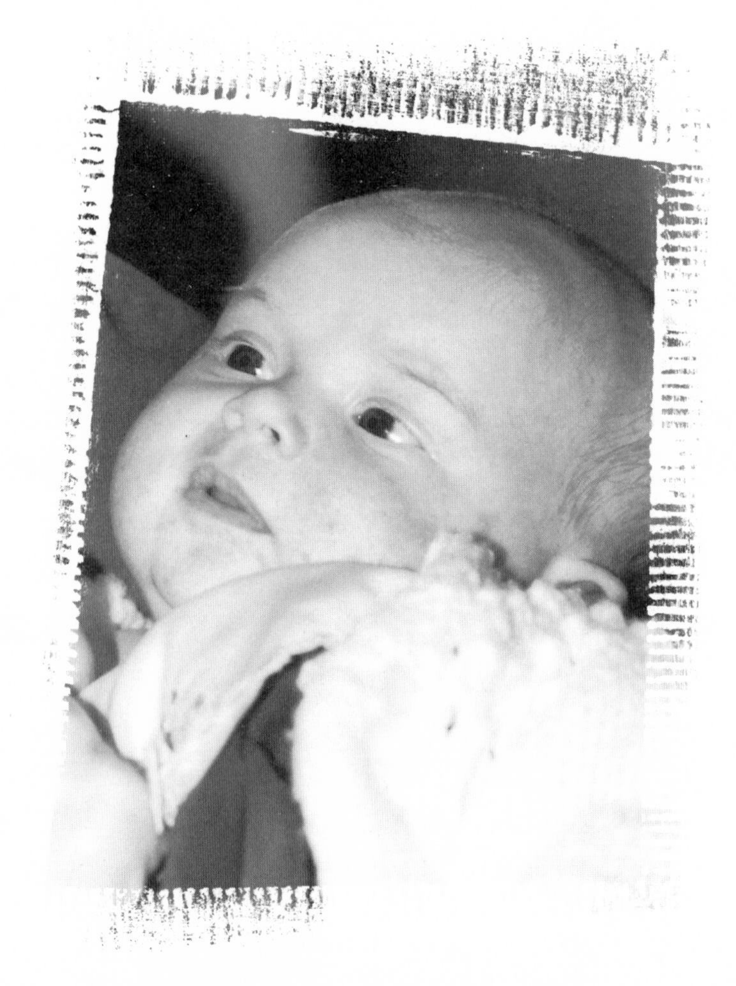

Acknowledgements

Writing books is a lot like having children. Both take a lot of work and time. Both are, in some ways, risky propositions.

This book is the loving fruit of the marriage my husband Andrew and I have built for the past twenty years. Having children and raising them are the great adventure we share. It has changed us and continues to shape our lives. Andrew, though your name is rarely mentioned, for me you are present on every page.

Expecting a Miracle would not have been possible without the fine art of excellent editors. My thanks go to Molly Rosa and Sister Madonna Ratliff, FSP. Your insightful guidance brought the best out of me, and made *Expecting a Miracle* better than I ever hoped.

I thank, too, my long time friend and elder brother in Christ, Fr. Paul Henry. He brought me—kicking and screaming—to the works of St. Francis De Sales. Because of you, Father, I have learned to "live Jesus" in the present moment of family life.

Finally, I am grateful to all my children. Jana, Nadja, baby Paul, Kolbe, Katerina, Kyril, Austin, Juliana, and Marjeta, all my love is for each one of you. You have brought me to the shores of divine mystery. You are the wind in my sails. May Jesus bring all of us safely to his harbor.

Contents

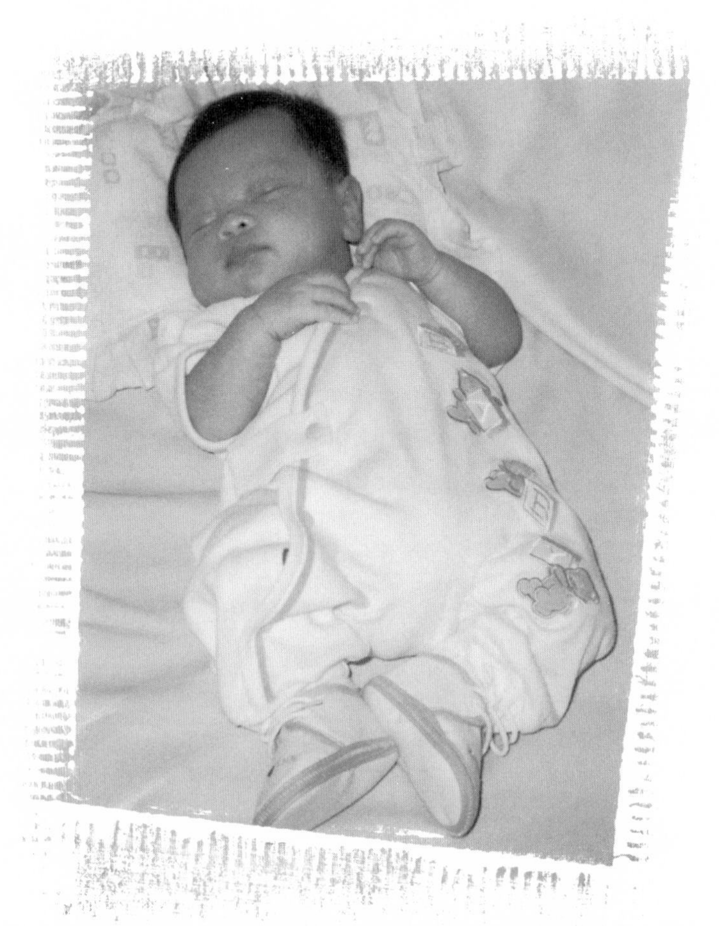

Introduction

For women, pregnancy and motherhood are a joyful and exciting time of life. Yet, at the same time, motherhood is probably one of the deepest and darkest unknowns. A leap of faith here affects a woman for her entire lifetime—and perhaps beyond. In addition, maternity in the modern world has become an increasingly complicated proposition. On the one hand there lies the challenge of what can seem like the all-consuming demands of motherhood, including the struggle of developing and using our own gifts within the context of mothering. On the other hand, our expectations can be clouded by the sheer number of options for our life or career. As women become more self-assured, we may find ourselves feeling less sure about everything else. We are uncomfortably stretched between life within the home and life outside of it. In our search for striking the proper balance, at times our lives have all the grace of an elephant walking a tightrope.

For many women maternity has become a matter of whether, when, and how much. Nevertheless, pregnancy and childbirth have remained the sun that rises and sets on the feminine horizon. Motherhood is the essence of womanhood. We live it out in some way whether we bear biological children or not. Women know the transformative power of maternity in our physical and emotional lives. Yet few of us draw deeply enough from this power to find what pregnancy and childbirth can teach us about our spiritual selves.

For the Christian woman, reflection on pregnancy and childbirth can be the point of departure for a rich meditation on discipleship and the life of faith. The expanding womb is not only the dwelling place of a life before birth, but a living invitation to expand one's heart for the Life who is in every way as dynamic and real as the unborn child. The child in utero is a living icon of the indwelling Spirit of God. Pregnancy is a parable of how we experience God's presence, and how divine life shows itself in us.

Many Catholics would be quick to point out that Mary, the Virgin Mother of God, is the feminine model of faith and the disciple par excellence. This truth is beyond dispute. But what many of us have done by insisting on placing the Blessed Mother so high on a pedestal that no one could hope to follow in her steps has not served our own spiritual growth well. By doing this, we do not allow Mary to lead by example. We have abstracted Mary by tearing her away from the emotional and spiritual constants of motherhood that all the rest of us experience. We have clothed her in a garment of faith without doubt, trust without fear, and joy without anxiety. Meanwhile, we are wrapped in all these rags, always hoping that no one will pull a thread hard enough to unravel us to complete exposure.

Other faith traditions often do just the opposite, giving Mary little attention at all. Consequently, many view Mary as spiritually, if not functionally, irrelevant to God's plan of salvation. Whether highlighted or disregarded, somehow Mary's personal faith journey is ignored. The only fruit of her pregnancy we seem to recognize is the child Jesus. But in the everyday experience of women who bear children, each pregnancy bears not only a child, but a new spiritual dimension.

Because it is a journey toward new life, pregnancy is by nature a pilgrimage, not a hermitage. The existence of an unborn child means that the pregnant woman is never truly alone—she is always "with child." Indeed, pregnancy is not meant to be a time of seclusion, but rather a joyful sharing of all it means to be present, to be together.

Upon learning that Elizabeth had conceived in her old age, Luke tells us that Mary "went with haste to the hill country of Judea, to the house of Zechariah." In that visit lies the most compelling Scriptural example of women sharing faith. For both of these women, the common feminine experience of maternity brings into focus the powerful life-giving Spirit of God.

We expect the miraculous in birth. We do so, however, realizing that the process of expecting *is itself* a miracle. *Expecting a Miracle* is written in this spirit. Its purpose is to provide the reader with an opportunity to see in pregnancy a model and image of spiritual growth. In sharing Mary's walk through pregnancy, we can come—as she did—to a deeper well of faith. Through personal anecdotes and reflection, *Expecting a Miracle* is intended to create an experience of visitation not just between reader and author, but also between the reader and Mary, and, ultimately, Jesus Christ.

Chapter 1

Before I Knew You Were, You Were There

Discovering that you are pregnant

> Before I formed you in the womb I knew you, and before you were born I consecrated you...
>
> Jeremiah 1:5

I'll never forget the first "annunciation" in my life. I certainly wasn't visited by an angel, but somehow the experience of being made aware of a new life within me had that taste of awesome mystery nonetheless. I was twenty-two, married only six months, and living far away from any family. I had not yet had much time to make friends. I remember being embarrassed to take the home pregnancy test up to the drugstore cashier. I kept thinking that everyone was watching me and wondering.

Do-it-yourself pregnancy tests were relatively new then, and they weren't very easy to perform or read. It was hard to tell if there really was a little ring at the bottom of the test tube. It was even harder to believe that swirling chemicals could have any relationship whatsoever to a baby being born.

I felt startled and caught completely off-guard by that positive test result. Just as if I had walked into a surprise party, I was at once thrilled and terrified. I wondered if this was all really happening to me. Somehow, it didn't seem possible that I was going to be somebody else's mommy. I didn't feel pregnant, or look pregnant. The only evidence I had was that ring in the test tube, and the fact that I was a week late.

For me, the thought of having children was abstract and theoretical—and therefore, distant enough to be safe. In the hypothetical, having a baby would be nice. It was something I would want sometime in the future. All of a sudden, I had fast-forwarded into the future. The future was happening now.

A million questions flooded my thoughts. How did this happen (as if I didn't know!)? Would it be a boy or a girl? Was the baby healthy? When was I due? Just how much was this going to hurt? What doctor would I go to? How was this all going to change my life? What were people, especially my family, going to say? What kind of mother would I be? What kind of father would my husband be? The frosting on the cake was the frightening realization that I had absolutely no idea how to care for a baby. I was an only child who had never liked baby-sitting very much.

I felt tangled in contradictory emotions. Part of me wanted to go out and buy maternity clothes, learn how to knit, and shout my news to anyone who would listen. But there was also a sizable place in me where fear resided—fear that fed the desire to keep it all a secret and the gnawing doubt that any of this was real.

We've all had the experience of being startled by someone who seems to appear suddenly from nowhere. Unaware of another's presence, we go right along as if we're alone. The person may be with us for quite awhile, but the instant we first notice it can really give us a jolt.

I remember having the sense at the beginning of each of my pregnancies that my unborn child had somehow crept up on me. I was dumbfounded at the thought that this new person had been silently—and secretly—growing inside me. It really is amazing that before any of us knows we are pregnant, indeed, before we even suspect it, the tiny life we carry within us is already there.

In much the same way, sensing the divine finger tapping us on the shoulder can startle and unsettle us. God's very existence challenges our complacency and reminds us that we are not in control. God's presence—once we have perceived it—asks us to respond.

When we realize that God is there, we can feel disoriented. It is as if we had awakened to find ourselves in a strange room after a long sleep.

It's reassuring to know that Mary had doubts and questions too. When the angel appeared, she must have wondered if she was seeing things. I always imagine her gasping at the sight and sound of him. The Scriptures record him saying "Fear not," not because it sounded poetic, but because Mary was truly afraid. To be sure, if the angel's appearance was startling, no doubt his words to her were even more so.

Hearing his message that she would bear a son, Mary's first response is the natural and immediate question, "How can this be?" Gabriel is quick to tell her of the overshadowing power of God, but adds the news of Elizabeth's pregnancy as well. Despite Elizabeth's barrenness and old age, and regardless of Mary's virginity, both have conceived; as the angel proclaims, "Nothing is impossible with God." Perhaps mystified, Mary gives her consent. She commits her humanity—questions and all—to God's plan.

The Scriptures tell us that Mary "set out and went with haste to a Judean town in the hill country, where she entered the house of Zechariah and greeted Elizabeth" (Lk 1:39). The journey was a long one, and doubtless took a few days. What a blend of excitement and anxiety she must have had in her heart. Like all of us at the beginning, Mary probably didn't feel pregnant. She had no symptoms, no medical test result, no proof of any kind that what the angel told her was true. That is, if the angel really had appeared. She may well have questioned if she had dreamt the whole thing up. Or worse yet, perhaps there was reason to doubt the source of what she saw. To make the journey meant that Mary would have to trust and abandon herself to the meaning of the angel's words. She *had* to go to see her cousin. She *had* to know. Insofar as it was possible, she *had* to be sure.

When Mary saw Elizabeth, radiant and blooming in her sixth month, she knew the reality of her own pregnancy. Elizabeth testified to Mary's maternity, saying, "And why has this happened to me, that the mother of my Lord comes to me?" (Lk 1:43) The source of Elizabeth's knowledge of Mary's child is kept secret from us. It's clear the two women had much to talk about in those three months.

Like the presence of the child in the womb, the presence of God is not dependent on our awareness. We may not have any sense of God's presence, any more than we do of an embryo growing within us. Still, God is with us all along. In the absence of any evidence, God is there. Before we are conscious of anything or anyone beyond our own existence, God is there. Even when we are wrapped up in the cloud of ourselves to the exclusion of all else, God is there with us. We may disregard or think God irrelevant—even nonexistent. We can lose sight of God's presence in our lives, or simply forget that we are not alone. God is there nonetheless, silently and secretly present with us, and growing to stretch and fill whatever space in our lives we allow.

Lord God, how wonderful it is that before I knew anything about you, you were there. You are everywhere around me, like the air I breathe—too small to be seen and too big to be grasped.

Throughout my life, you have made your presence known to me in countless ways. Forgive me for the many times I've been so caught up in myself that I haven't even noticed you.

Awaken and startle me, Lord. Give my heart eyes and ears of faith. Let me see that you are never just "there," but always "here." Let me hear your voice as the silence beneath the noise. Help me to perceive your presence within me, within all hearts who seek you, and even in those who don't.

Teach me how to be as present to you as you are to me, and let my life announce your presence to all the world. Amen.

Chapter 2

The Stranger Inside Me

Accepting the one-of-a-kind gift of your child

> For now we see in a mirror, dimly, but then we will see face to face. Now I know only in part; then I will know fully, even as I have been fully known.
>
> 1 Corinthians 13:12

Most people would say that it's impossible to love someone you don't even know. I've often wondered, however, if it isn't even more difficult to love someone you *do* know! I remember thinking about my unborn children as strangers, wondering not only what they would look like, but what they would *be* like. Watching for their personalities to emerge was very much like waiting for the curtain to go up at a theater. I couldn't write the script or even cast the actors. I was only the audience.

Our oldest daughter was a real shock to my system. She loved dolls and tea parties and frilly dresses. She was naturally graceful, exhibited a full-blown maternal instinct practically from birth, and was adept at charming whatever she wanted out of unsuspecting adults. I remember her crying her eyes out when she was just over a year old because I hadn't done her hair the way she wanted it. She was—and pretty much still is—the quintessential *femme fatale.* Sometimes I've caught myself wondering where she came from. She is so very different from me!

Our second child, however, is in every way a chip off my block. Watching her is like looking in a time-warped mirror. She is assertive and direct, but extremely sensitive and big-hearted. She has a keen sense of fairness, is rather hot-tempered, and has a contagious laugh. When she walks into a room, she is noticed immediately. She just sparkles.

Nearly everyone we know has remarked to us about how very different our two oldest girls are from each other. They really are like night and day, as distinct as the breakfasts they used to eat when they were small (one had dry toast and grapefruit, while the other delighted in Lucky Charms). Living with them and watching them become more of who they are every day has been a real adventure.

Any parent of more than one child will attest to the fact that no baby is a "blank check." Each is unique, irreplaceable, and unrepeatable. (Some days, that in itself is a comfort!) This reality became even clearer to us with the birth of our first son. I had never really believed those mothers who kept trumping up the differences between boys and girls. I suppose that I suspected it was all just an excuse for making "boys will be boys" the rule of the house. And boy, was I wrong. After three sons and five daughters, I hate to admit just how much.

In raising my children, I've come to the conclusion that the bottom line of gender differences is a matter of "language." For boys, actions don't speak louder than words—actions *are* words. Boys express themselves and interact with each other in almost pure body language. They are constantly touching each other. Everything physical—a pat on the head, a tug on the jacket—is understood. Often what is spoken is barely heard. Girls, on the other hand, speak a far more relational language. They are careful to reinforce relationships and define roles. Girls are attentive to their own feelings as well as others'. Placing great emphasis on things like tone of voice and facial expressions, girls are always trying to read between the lines. Many of them consider *how* something is said or what is left unsaid more important than what is actually stated. The challenge for every mother and father is to become "bilingual."

The truth is that when we carry a baby, we are carrying a one-of-a-kind individual whom we choose to love regardless of who he or she is. We have absolutely no control over the kind of people who will call us "mommy." Even with all our advanced medical testing, we cannot know what our children will be like or even if we will find it easy to like them. Many times I have marveled at the fact that if it were left completely up to me, I may not have chosen the people who are my own children to be my friends! But differences need not be obstacles to love.

Who your children are is as much a mystery as who they will become. Differences between children are evident even before birth. One child is quiet, another is active in the womb. One responds to music, another to a change in position. One stretches, and another kicks so hard that it is difficult to sleep. Newborns are unique too. Our first child was content and serene, our second was a bit feisty, our third was acutely observant, our fourth was very cuddly, and so on.

Initially, I had all kinds of expectations of what babies were supposed to be like. I was often aggravated and annoyed by some of my children's personality traits, which grated against my own. In some ways, I still am. But by the time we had our third child, the way I thought about babies had changed. With a little more patience and understanding, I became a bit more willing to bend to who they were, rather than impose upon them who I wanted them to be. I began to see them as individuals caught, for a time, in babyhood. As such, I saw that my primary task was not to mold them, but rather to help them emerge and develop into more of what God—not I—had created them to be.

Eventually, it began to dawn on me that God had placed these particular children in my life to help me emerge too. It isn't a one-way street. Actually, it's a lot more like a large traffic circle with spokes going out in every direction. We have as much to gain *from* our children as we have to give *to* them. Each member of a family influences everyone else. There are things we can only learn from living with each other. Love challenges us all not only to overlook what we may not like in another, but to rejoice in those things that are different. My children couldn't choose their Mommy, just as I couldn't choose my children. But God has chosen us for each other. For better or worse—and that *is* what is up to us!—we are all stuck with each other.

We all like to think that we are the ones doing the choosing. But Jesus made it all very clear when he said to his disciples, "You did not choose me but I chose you" (Jn 15:16). Mary and Jesus were chosen for each other. Neither one of them would have become the fullest of who they were meant to be without the other. From all the women who ever lived, God chose Mary. The Almighty created her not only to bear Jesus, but to mother him.

I can't begin to imagine what it would be like knowing that the child I carried was the Son of God, can you? Mary had a great deal to wonder about. What would her Son be like—what could he be like? Would he run and play like other children, or be some sort of dreamy-eyed loner? What evidence might there be that he wasn't human only? But then, he would be human after all, wouldn't he? And how would this Divine Son—the Chosen, the Anointed, the Promised One—how would this child grow up under her authority? We all ask ourselves somewhere along the line if we are good enough to be the mothers of our children. Mary, too, had to ask herself whether she'd be up to this; indeed, whether anyone could. And as she pondered, the Divine Stranger, the Son of God mysteriously her Son as well, secretly made his home within her.

To God there are no strangers, for the Creator has made us all. God chooses to love us, not *because* God knows us or *in spite* of knowing us, but because we are his. To us, God is the ever-present stranger. Like unborn children growing inside us, God is always with us. There is a certain affinity that attracts us to the Holy One. But like each child we bear, what we know is greatly outweighed by what we do not, even cannot, know. Nonetheless, God remains intimate, at the very heart of our hearts. There is nothing that stands between us; nothing that keeps us from each other. God is who God is—that is even his name. We cannot change the Unchanging One, or mold the Rock who saves us, even though at times divinity may grate against us. We can only help God to emerge in our lives *as God*. And we do so knowing that we become most fully ourselves in the presence of the Holy One.

Lord , although you are always with me, I hardly know you! You are closer than close, and yet very much a stranger to me. I've not yet even scratched the surface of all that you are; and yet you know everything there is to know about me.

Sometimes you frighten me, Lord, because you are too great and powerful. And sometimes, you frighten me because you are too small and weak. I know that I have tried to mold and change you—instead of allowing you to mold and change me. I have wanted to make you more comfortable for me to be with.

Teach me, Lord, to embrace the mystery that you are—both the magnificence and the meekness—as well as the echo of that mystery in me. Help me give you my heart so you can emerge in my life in freedom and fullness. Amen.

Chapter 3

Intimacy and the Walls Within

Bonding before birth

> For I am convinced that neither death, nor life, nor angels, nor rulers, nor things present, nor things to come, nor powers, nor height, nor depth, nor anything else in all creation, will be able to separate us from the love of God in Christ Jesus our Lord.
>
> Romans 8:38–39

It's funny how, all at once, someone can seem both present and distant. In my own life I know that being there doesn't necessarily mean *being there*. Sometimes my thoughts, anxieties, or preoccupations have led me out of wherever I am and away from whomever I'm with to a dreamy place where nothing can reach me. Whatever is happening continues in my apparent presence, when in all truth I'm a million miles away, functionally absent from everything around me.

When I have been pregnant, all that dreaminess seemed to intensify. On the one hand, I'm absorbed by the reality of a new life within, constantly making plans and thinking things through. But on the other hand, all those thoughts and plans seem to focus more on myself than on the child. It is as if he or she was coming, but had not yet truly come.

For me, pregnancy has always been an experience of being pulled between the "already" and the "not yet." The child growing inside me always seemed so very far away. Closer than close, not only *with* me, but *within* me, I have still felt as if my child either didn't exist or wasn't truly mine. At the same time, I knew that there was no distance between me and my unborn baby. There was nothing to separate, nothing to keep the two of us apart. The very nature of pregnancy made us completely present to each other, and intimately so. The wall of the womb is a thin one. The walls of the heart, however, can be another story.

I didn't have any difficulty bonding with our first two children. From the moment I knew of their existence, I experienced deep feelings for them. My third pregnancy was much the same. I quickly invested all my maternal emotional stock into my new baby. But the pregnancy abruptly ended in a miscarriage. There were so many loose ends left dangling. So many unfulfilled expectations. One day everything was fine, and the next day nothing was. I don't think the words "shock" or "trauma" go too far in describing what it was like.

I really wanted another child, and when I became pregnant again six months later, I was elated. Nonetheless, I found myself consciously refusing to become emotionally attached before reaching the second trimester. I held back my deepest love and affection toward my son at the start, because I was afraid of losing him. I still felt the loss of my miscarriage. Instead of intimacy, I chose to allow my fear of losing another child to prompt my emotional defenses. I treated his very existence as tentative. I did not open my whole heart to him until I felt secure. In so doing, I did not fully recognize him as a person. Rather, I saw him as something that was *mine*—something I could lose. This was understandable, in light of what I had been through.

Although there are no physical barriers to intimacy during pregnancy, emotional and spiritual walls can and do create distance between mothers and their unborn children. These interior walls can be almost anything. Fear, stress, ambivalence, hurt, shame—even joy and pride—can get in the way of our treating our unborn babies as persons in their own right rather than as mere extensions of ourselves. There is rarely a problem making enough room in our bodies for a new baby, but making room in our hearts and in our lives requires more of us.

Intimacy depends on each person treating the other *as a person.* We cannot be intimate with things. Similarly, we cannot be intimate with a thought or a wish or a *potential* person. Intimacy, wherever it exists, is between persons. It is precisely this sharing of our humanity and our unique personhood that makes the bonds of deep love possible.

When the angel Gabriel asked Mary if she would bear the Son of God, he was asking her not only to share her humanity with her child, as all mothers must, but to give humanity itself to God. When the Word became flesh, it was Mary's flesh he took to do so. In order to dwell among us, he first had to dwell within her. God became Mary's—her very own Son—so that we could all become his.

God's intimate bond with us in Christ began with the intimacy shared with Mary. She did not allow any interior walls in her heart to keep the Lord at a distance or to limit the Holy Spirit's movement in her life. God freely shared divinity with Mary as she shared her humanity with God. God took up residence in her womb in the same way that he had already made a home in her heart.

Through Mary, God acquired the humanity shared with us in Jesus, so that the Holy One might become intimate with us as he did with her. God invites us to closeness beyond measure. Our God asks us to allow him beyond the walls within our hearts that keep him away from us, even though God dwells within us. God is simultaneously light-years away and closer to us than the air we breathe. God has no interior walls to keep us from his heart. And because God is not an idea, a thing, or a wish—because God is *personal*—the intimacy the Lord has chosen with us is possible when we respond by choosing to be close to him.

O God, my God, there is nothing that can separate me from your love. You assure me that all I have to do to find you is to seek you. You tell me that if I listen, I will hear you knocking. You promise that if I open my heart to you, you will indeed come in. But Lord, I often choose to keep you at a distance. Sometimes without even knowing it, I give you part of myself, but not all. I draw lines in the sand of my soul and tell you not to cross them. And when you offer me more, sometimes I tell you that I would rather have less. I keep you in a box large enough to hold closely what I desire from you, but small enough to prevent you from getting too close to what you desire from me.

Tear down the walls in my heart that limit your love. Teach me to surrender not only what I want to give, but what you long for me to receive from you. Show me that you do not approach to destroy or hurt me, but to embrace and comfort me. Help me to know that because you are Love, you seek me out; that because you created me for union, you pursue me. Amen.

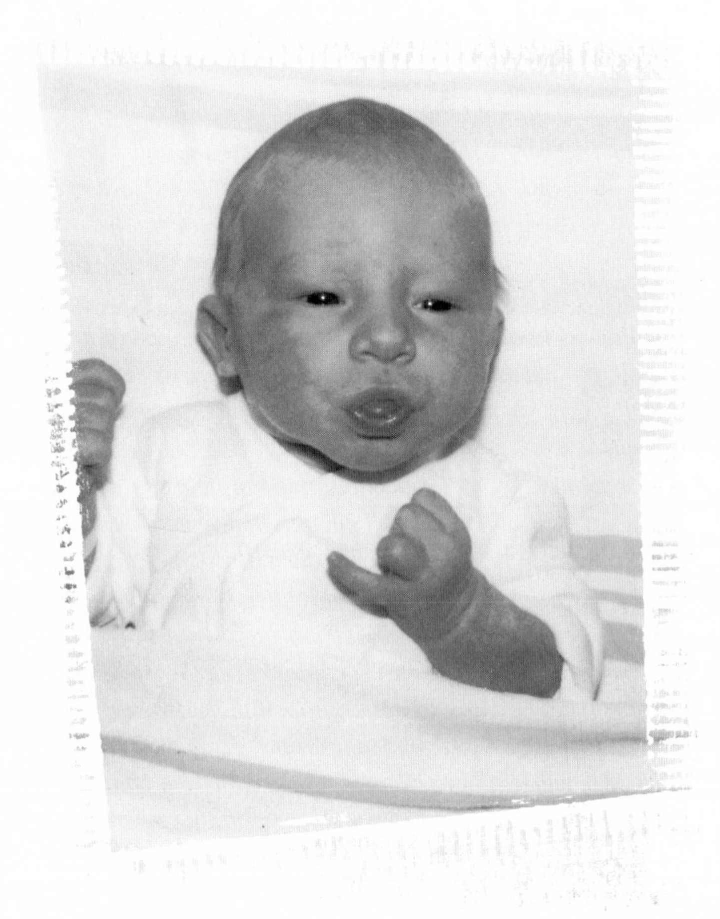

Chapter 4

The Best Laid Plans...

Surrendering control

> For surely I know the plans I have for you...plans for your welfare and not for harm, to give you a future with hope.
> Jeremiah 29:11

Our culture applauds both the desire and the ability to control our own destinies. We are taught to emulate people who know what they want and get it, even if it means treating life more like an investment portfolio than a gift. I have to admit that I have fit quite comfortably into that mold. I've always had high and well-defined goals, and have been successful in reaching them in large part because I orchestrate my efforts effectively. I have seen many others, far more able than myself, fail to achieve what they set out to do simply because they did not plan well or were unable to stick to a plan they had made.

Babies have a way of interfering with our plans. Of our first four children, three were not "planned"—at least, not by us. The first one came too quickly after we were married, and the second too quickly after the first. The four years that followed were a frequent battleground between my husband and myself over whether or not to have a third child. He wanted more, and I was happy with the way things were, not to mention scared of what things might become with more than two children in the house. After putting up a good fight (and growing up a bit), I warmed to the idea, only to then miscarry. Finally, our *very planned* son was born. Our fourth child came right on his heels only seventeen months later.

I know that when I'm not expecting to be expecting and suddenly find myself pregnant, my whole world is thrown for a loop. It has seemed to me at times that just when I've been ready to move on with my own life, I got pregnant. I have cried lots of tears over these "interruptions." But in retrospect, I laugh when I think that literally every time I called for an application to graduate school—law, liberal arts, fine arts, or theology—I had yet another baby. For a while I gave up making such phone calls. After the birth of our seventh child, I started a master's degree program anyway.

Those were years of both intense struggle and pivotal growth. The truth is that the most difficult things about raising several children have little to do with the cooking and cleaning, the steady stream of laundry that has to be done, or even meeting the never-ending expenses. The real challenges are all about attitudes, resentments, fears, and selfishness. Eventually, I reached the decision to stop trying to control life and, instead, to manage life as it unfolds. Bringing the next four children home was much easier. The key to that change was recognizing that my life wasn't just my *own* anymore. It had become a life together, a *shared* life to which we all give and from which we have all most richly received.

Looking back, I better understand why I chose to take the road I did. After two children in quick succession, I became convinced that if any of us—read "I"—was going to get what we wanted out of life, we needed to take control of this reproduction thing. At that time in our lives we used contraceptives to avoid another pregnancy until further notice. When my husband finally won me over to having another baby, we dropped the contraceptives and started "trying."

Once the decision was made, having a third child seemed like a simple proposition. It had been all too easy to conceive before, so I was sure that all I had to do was throw caution to the winds. Two months later, I was pregnant. Everything fell into place according to schedule—until I miscarried. I had had about as much success trying to have a baby as I'd had trying to avoid one. What a shock it was to discover that despite my strategizing and careful execution, I was powerless over the outcome. Reality crashed head-on into the illusion that I was in control. It felt like my whole world was shattered in pieces. The most terrifying thing of all was the possibility that if I wasn't in control then maybe no one was. Suddenly everything seemed random and disordered.

I had been so sure that control would keep things from getting too complicated; that it would free us from all sorts of undesirable circumstances. But I had never considered what I would do if this approach failed. Too much depended on my being in total control—way too much for the small amount of control I found I had. Somewhere along the way I had lost the very freedom I was trying to gain. I had become trapped by the plans I myself had made. I had begun to act as if I believed that we were the only ones actively involved in our reproductive lives. I was wrong.

None of this is to say that we should be *reckless* or *irresponsible*. To the contrary, the life of faith is a loving *response*, an openness to God. There may be times when this openness leads to a decision to wait before having a child. In the context of a living relationship with God, spacing births is qualitatively different from closing one's self off to God's gift of another child. Christian spouses walk a narrow moral and spiritual way between a contraceptive mentality on one side and imprudence on the other.

Our God is a God of creativity and initiative. Whether or not we have anticipated having a child at a particular time, God has plans for us and for our children. The difficulty comes when our plans conflict with God's. Many people of faith talk about embracing God's will. But when it comes to the big areas of our lives, like childbearing, few of us trust God enough to allow the Master's plans to take precedence over our own. Unfortunately, many of us think it easier to spend our lives wrestling with the angel, rather than listening, let alone responding to his message.

Mary did not expect to become the mother of Christ. Certainly, it was not her ambition to be young, unmarried, and unexpectedly pregnant. Yet even in the moment that sin entered the world through the human heart, God planned salvation to enter it through a virgin's womb. Jesus was God's plan—not hers, not ours.

I'm sure that if Mary had studied God's plan, it would have appeared ill-conceived. Under the law of Moses, the penalty for breaking a marriage betrothal and becoming pregnant with another man's child was death. From a merely human point of view, the wisdom of sending the messiah in this way was questionable at best.

But Mary didn't evaluate God's plan: she didn't argue with it or seek to alter it in any way. The details she knew, frightening as they must have been, did not prompt her to judge the plan itself. Mary was not the kind of person to put her trust in any plan. She found God alone worthy of such trust. What Mary needed to know was *whose* plan this was. If it was God's, that would be enough.

All of us find that kind of trust difficult. Perhaps Mary did too, but she trusted God with her whole life anyway. If only more of us could choose to do the same more often. Wanting to be responsible and free, many of us willingly take upon ourselves the heavy burden of deciding if, when, and how many children we will bear. But while we seek to plan our families, we can easily forget that God is planning an eternal family too. We shut God out when we treat our lives like sole-proprietorships instead of joint ventures.

But as we grow in faith, we stumble over the limits of our own reasoning and control. Eventually trust must overcome fear, and obedience must take the place of willfulness. I often marvel at how the life I now lead looks precious little like the one I had planned. I know too, when I look into the faces of my children, that if it had been left up to me alone, some of them would never have been born. In those reflective moments, I thank God for taking initiative in my life.

Whether or not you have a house or money in the bank, and whether or not you feel particularly ready to be a parent, there is no "good time" to have a child. There will always be sacrifices to make, and a "planned" child will not necessarily be loved more than an "unplanned" one. Our children have taught me that "unplanned" doesn't have to mean *un*wanted or *un*loved. It's all in how we choose to respond.

It's easy to slip into thinking of new life, or children, as something *we* should and must plan. Yet there is great freedom in realizing that there is Someone else who is participating in the planning. There is joy too, in allowing God to work without an argument. The freedom I thought would come with artificial contraception came only when we decided to abandon it permanently. Without it, we have left the door open to *God's* initiative. As "in control" as I like to be, I have seen that when I have given up trying to design my own life, I have never been disappointed. It is because no matter how good my plans may be, God's are always better.

O great God of all creation, you have designed all the universe even to the smallest detail. You have placed each star and each blade of grass. From your hand comes every living thing; not even a sparrow falls from flight without you knowing it. And Lord, you have designed each one of us for a purpose. You have plans not just for some, but for all; plans filled with hope and love.

But Lord, I have plans of my own. I spend most of what you have given me to fulfill my own wants and desires. Although I have asked you many times to help me set a course, I have rarely allowed you to take the wheel. I have often invited you along the paths I have chosen, but have seldom asked you to do the choos-

ing. I have sought your blessing, but not always your will.

Lord, let my life's ambition be to please you. Help me to surrender my life into your hands. Set me like a precious stone in the place you have designed for me, near all the other jewels you have placed in my life. Give me the grace to fulfill the purpose for which you have created me and to give glory to your name. Amen.

Chapter 5

Oh No! Not Again!

Embracing your fertility

> [Children] are indeed a heritage from the Lord,
> the fruit of the womb a reward.
> Like arrows in the hand of a warrior
> are the [children] of one's youth.
> Happy is the man who has
> his quiver full of them.
>
> Psalm 127:3–5

When I found out I was pregnant the second time, our first child was ten months old. I knew that I would want at least one more child, though it seemed a bit early. But I wondered how in the world I was going to handle two babies. The best I could do was resign myself to coping. It frightened me to think that I was only twenty-three and that I had lot of childbearing years ahead of me. At this rate, I thought, I could be single-handedly responsible for overpopulating my neighborhood. That was a distinction I wanted no part of.

To tell you the truth, the first six months after our second daughter's birth are a blur to me even now. I was absolutely overwhelmed and found that going from one to two was as big an adjustment as going from zero to one. The work wasn't that difficult, but learning to manage the relationship *between* children and my own building stress was. I was so frazzled and inept at moving quickly between their needs that disasters just seemed to be a way of life. I remember putting the baby down to discover that my toddler had exploited the irresistible opportunity to put an entire jar of Vaseline in her hair. Of course, it *had* to be the day we had an appointment with the pediatrician. So much for appearances!

I'm glad to say that things did get better—rather, I got better at holding everything together, if tenuously at times. After the initial shock of having to split my attention and energies between children, I found that they really did entertain and teach each other. As our family has continued to grow, I can admit that in some ways it is easier to have eight now than it was to have those first two. We were all each other's guinea pigs in a makeshift laboratory of family life. Sometimes we got a little more broken than broken-in.

Consequently, at the time I kept fighting the notion of having another baby. As I told my husband repeatedly, I was not about to be the vehicle for fulfilling what I called his "Abraham complex," that is, his desire to be the father of many nations. I, for one, thought two was enough (some days, more than enough!), and that enough was enough. More would have definitely been too much.

But when our son was born a few years later, I found to my surprise that having another child was quite simple, hardly an interruption to our household at all. However, when he was only eight months old, lightning struck again. All I could do was panic. My husband had lost his job three months before. The house we were living in was too small. We already had three children in one bedroom, and our bedroom was being used as a temporary office for my husband's fledgling business. We didn't have the time, the space, or the money for yet another child. We didn't have medical insurance either. I couldn't escape the anxiety of wondering what in the world would happen to us.

What did actually happen was astonishing: nothing. *Nothing much happened!* We ended up living in our six room, one bathroom house not just with four children, but with six. Sleeping arrangements evolved continually. For a while, one of our children slept with my mother, who also lives with us. At another time we had two sets of bunk beds and a crib in one room. When we were completely out of space, we closed off the dining room and made it into a bedroom for our oldest girls. We struggled, but we managed. My husband returned to the security of a normal job after three years on his own. And finally we were able to pay off the hospital bill for the birth of our fourth child and buy a bigger house. While all my worst fears never really materialized, something quite wonderful did. God added, and continued to add, more beautiful children to our family.

Caring for a large family is not nearly so difficult as I anticipated. After all, no one can do more than the day will hold. Larger families have a different dynamic than smaller ones. The older children help more than you'd think, and the younger ones don't stay young for very long. By the time we had our fourth child, I had begun to hit a rhythm with it. We named her after St. Catherine of Siena, the youngest of twenty-five children. Just think how much poorer we would all be if her parents had called it quits at twenty-four!

I have to admit breaking out into a cold sweat when our oldest child dedicated a story she had written in school to the hope she would become the eldest of ten. But when we had four children, I came to terms with the possibility that I might not end up with just four. I resisted looking at myself as a mother-of-four and accepted that it wouldn't take much to become a mother-of-more. In time, that acceptance became joy.

"Fertile" is part of who we are, as well as a vehicle for us to become who we are meant to be. But fully embracing our fertility means accepting and responding rather than trying to anticipate and control. Fruitfulness is broader and deeper than the mere physical ability to have children. It is a spiritual openness to loving others that results in an almost miraculous multiplication of blessing. In this sense, the family itself is fertile. The welcoming household is rich earth, plowed and prepared for unconditional love and acceptance.

Watching our now eight children arrive and grow up together, I can't imagine our lives without any one of them. Every person contributes far more than he or she consumes. Because each child has something to offer, our whole family is enriched. We have all learned a little something about ballet, fencing, airplanes, Civil War history, dinosaurs, Irish step dancing, and Russia. We have gained an appreciation of how to live with and love all sorts of people: impulsive, energetic, introspective—you name it. Even more, we have each discovered things about ourselves simply by sharing life intimately with a rich assortment of others.

The wonder of the Lord is that he never stops creating. God is a master of multiplication. The Creator does it not only in Bible stories, like that of the loaves and fishes, but in our lives as well. God is always doing something new, and always giving us something more of himself. The Divine Gardener is forever planting a new blessing, a new life, and a new gift in our souls. Divine life is *always* fertile.

Few of us would ever want God to stop bringing forth new fruits in our lives. But somehow, we always seem to want to limit our own fertility, both physical and spiritual. We rejoice in the experience of Christ's life in us, but somewhere along the line we might well catch ourselves wishing he would stop using us. We tell him in a hundred ways that enough is enough, that more is too much. We may even hope (secretly, of course!) that God would choose somebody else.

The Christian life of faith is a life always expectant. Indeed, the family of faith, the Church, is not exclusive or limited, but welcoming and expansive. We've all had the experience of being able to make room for one more at even the most crowded of dinner tables. It is in that way that the Father asks us to persevere in joy, to expand our hearts, and to open our lives to *all* the life he wishes to give to us—and through us. Fidelity and faith, however, is not a head count. It is a generous disposition of the heart. God invites us to look beyond our own struggles and see *each* child, *each* fruit of faithfulness and love, *each* new grace of discipleship as a unique gift divinely given.

O Lord, from the beginning your love overflowed into creation, and from nothingness you called all things into being. The universe is filled with your works. There is no one who could number them.

As wonderful as your creation is, sometimes I wish you would stop creating. Instead of allowing you a free hand in my life, I have sometimes fought to hold you back. I have struggled to withhold myself from you, saying, "Enough is enough! I've done my share!"

Lord, keep me in wonder at all you have made. Teach me to see all life as the unfolding of your creative and dynamic love. I give myself to you as an empty canvas to the master. Work your ways, O God, in the medium of my heart. Bring forth from my life all the fruit you desire, and, at your pleasure, create and recreate me in your love. Amen.

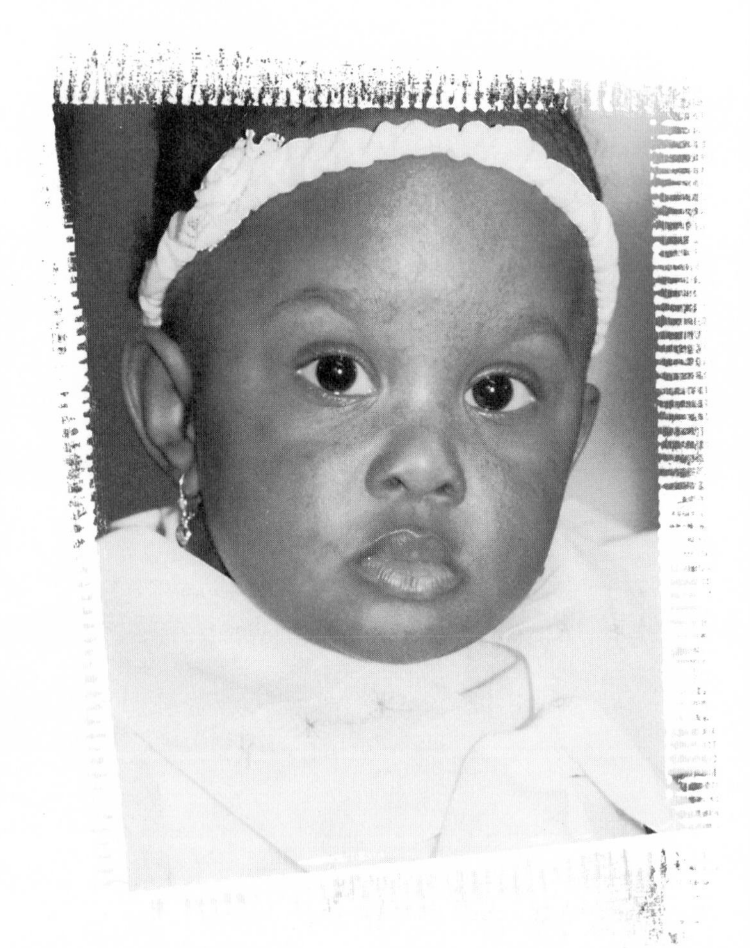

Chapter 6

The Quickening Spirit

Recognizing inner movements

As soon as I heard the sound of your greeting, the child in my womb leaped for joy.
Luke 1:44

Among the blessings of creation, I believe that there can be no greater pleasure than the sheer delight of feeling new life stir inside us. With each of my pregnancies I could hardly wait to feel the movements of my tiny stranger. I remember eagerly anticipating that small kick to catch my attention, especially when I was expecting for the first time.

One day during my first pregnancy, when I thought that all my morning sickness had finally come to an end, I suddenly felt a flutter, ever so slight, of what I supposed was indigestion. I recall going to the cupboard to get out the Coke syrup, fearing that nausea would ensue; but it never did. The next day, I felt that strange little quiver in my stomach again. About a week went by and I noticed that the flutter had become more frequent and perhaps a little stronger. It finally dawned on me that my "indigestion" was really my baby. Oops!

The movements became more insistent every day. The flutters became tickles; the tickles became thumps; the thumps became kicks. By the seventh month or so, I could actually *see* my baby move. I remember how startling it was to notice that my dress was jumping while I was talking with someone. It was almost as if my tiny child had something to add to the conversation.

With my more recent pregnancies the rest of the family has been quick to join in the fun. My older children even invented a prenatal game. They knocked and poked from the outside, and their new brother or sister would answer with a kick from the inside. My husband, on the other hand, has preferred a more sophisticated approach. He shined a flashlight on my stomach to elicit a response. The strange thing is, it worked!

Years ago it was thought that the first flutters in the womb signified that the child had "quickened" or suddenly come to life. Now we know that new life begins at the moment of conception, and that long before we can discern it, our tiny children are on the move. Knowing what to look for helped me tune in sooner. But even with lots of maternity experience under my ever-expanding belt, recognizing my baby's first movements was almost always very much after the fact. Only when the quivers became tiny kicks did I retroactively realize that those first subtle sensations were from my unborn child.

Most of us relish the wonder of such movements, playing in turn by answering a kick with a pat. It's amazing that long before we can see or touch our babies, let alone communicate with them, mother and child engage in a mysterious and unspoken dialogue of movement—a language filled with a vocabulary of twitches, kicks, and turns. The gift of pregnancy provides the stage for this living dance of maternal and fetal love.

These movements, when we become aware of them, immediately dispel any lingering doubts we may have about the reality that we are indeed carrying a new and distinct life. Every kick thrusts our unborn children further into our lives. These stirrings serve as a constant reminder that there is indeed a hidden life inside us that not only exists, but moves and grows.

The quickening movements of God in our lives are very much the same. Like the first tiny stirrings of our unborn children, we often don't know enough—or are too preoccupied—to notice the movements of the Spirit. But noticed or not, the living Spirit of God moves in our hearts. God's presence is neither figurative nor static. God is a living Being who is truly with us; who moves and grows in us like any other living being would. The Spirit may not move in our hearts in grand and sweeping strokes at first, but the Spirit *does* move.

God moves in our hearts and lives in a hundred thousand ways. Sometimes the Holy Spirit flutters the gentle reassurance of God's presence, and at other times kicks so hard that it hurts. God moves in both friends and adversaries, prodding and poking at our hearts in both peace and crisis. The Lord moves in happiness and in sorrow alike, for God is not inactive, but alive!

When it comes to the things of God, we all seem to expect everything to be on a scale larger-than-life. We think that we will feel God in thunder, power, and strength, and so we often miss the signs of his life within us that are quiet, small, and weak. As we grow in faith and experience, we learn to recognize these more gentle movements as the Lord's. The quivering of the Holy Spirit, however insignificant it may seem at the start, quicken in us the life of grace. That *always* causes quite a stir!

While pregnancy was a new adventure for Mary, the flutters, pokes, and kicks of the Lord were nothing new to her. She had felt his Spirit move in her heart long before she felt his tiny body move in her womb. His life had quickened so powerfully in her that God made her the vessel through which he would quicken all hearts.

As Mary felt this child of heaven, this Son of God, dance inside her, what unspeakable joy was hers! That same joy can belong to us as well. For like Mary, we can carry within us not only new human life, but Life—divine life, eternal life—itself.

Lord, it amazes me to think that you live so secretly in my heart that you remain hidden and mysterious even though you are within me.

Overwhelmed by the concerns of my own life, Lord, sometimes I don't even notice that your life is moving in my heart. Lulled by the rhythms of my earthly existence, I do not sense your dancing in my soul. But there are also times, Lord, when I think you kick too hard, times when your touch makes me wince.

Help me, Lord, to move with you. Stir up new life in my heart, O God, and quicken in me the fullness of your grace. Teach me to know your movements, however slight; and to accept them, however grand, that I may follow your every step with joy. Amen.

Chapter 7

Yours, Mine, and Ours

Fatherhood

> Therefore a man leaves his father and his mother and clings to his wife, and they become one flesh.
>
> Genesis 2:24

The ability to bring forth life lies at the heart of all that is uniquely feminine. No matter how involved a man is in pregnancy, childbirth, or parenting, he can never know what it's really like to bear a child. No man has ever had morning sickness or has had to waddle instead of walk. They may be empathetic and sensitive, expert Lamaze coaches, even obstetricians, but men will never fully understand what labor and delivery feel like. On the other hand, a man can never feel life stir within him. Just as he cannot personally know the pain of birth, neither can he know the joy that follows—a joy so deep that it overshadows pain. What a privilege it is to be a woman!

Maternity has been an all-absorbing experience for me. While my husband has remained well outside the world of the womb, I have been utterly consumed by pregnancy. Perhaps that's why I have found it quite tempting to think of my children as only *mine*, especially before they were born. After all, *I'm* the one who's pregnant; *I'm* the one who's doing all the work.

To me, it seemed that my husband treated pregnancy and childbirth as a spectator sport. Anyone who has ever seen a man at a baby shower knows what I mean when I say that he always appeared rather disconnected from the whole thing. He never seemed particularly attached to our children before they were born, and didn't spend much time speculating about gender, size, or temperament. His whole disposition was passive and irritatingly hands-off.

I had desperately wanted my husband to be a part of it all. Recognizing his limitations, I had always made great efforts to include him in each pregnancy with endless updates and running "play-by-play" commentary. Invariably, I grew frustrated with what I considered his lack of interest. No matter what I did, for him, pregnancy was nothing but a long wait.

I remember thinking one day how odd it was that my unborn child wasn't only mine; indeed, not even *mostly* mine. In truth, I wasn't just carrying *my* child.

I was carrying a living part of my husband inside me too. Both my husband and I were active participants and not passive bystanders.

What I never quite realized was that while my eyes were on the new baby, I was my husband's focus during pregnancy. Somehow, in the zeal of wanting my husband to share *my* experience, I had failed to recognize that he was having an experience all his own. In guarding, protecting, and providing for me, my husband was already exercising fatherly love. I was his link to our children before birth. I carried not only his physical connections to his child, but all the emotional and spiritual ones as well. In pregnancy I carried the child, but my husband in some sense carried me. With each successive pregnancy, I've come to see that although my husband will never know what it's like to be a mother, I will never fully appreciate what it means to be a father.

We can easily forget that our babies belong as much to their fathers as they do to us. No one would argue that maternity is limited to the physical or biological realms. But many of us overlook the counterpart of that truth. Paternity does not consist in merely supplying genetic material. There are spiritual and emotional components of being a father just as there are in being a mother. A man gives himself, all of who he is, to his child. In reality, our babies' fathers are not disconnected, but intimately attached to their unborn children.

I am reminded of fatherhood every time I look into the faces of our eight children. Few of them resemble me physically, especially when they were small. All of them look like my husband—even our adopted child! My children's faces show me that my maternity is bound up with his paternity. I would never be a mother if he were not a father. Children are the gifts of God that we give to one another.

Because no woman or man can bring forth new life alone, children are a living fulfillment of God's plan for both men and women: that in marriage, the two shall become one flesh. Children are the fruit of that oneness of spirit and of mind as well as of body. Each child is a perpetuation of that unity which exists not just for a passionate instant, but for eternity.

There is a difference between merely seeing new life as a gift and realizing it is a fruit. A gift is given by one and received by another, but a fruit grows from a loving relationship that is so intimate that it is both unitive and creative. Most of us are taught somewhere along the line that we should value life because it is a gift. But when Elizabeth cries out to Mary she says, "Blessed are you among women, and blessed is the fruit of your womb" (Lk 1:42). Jesus, the divine gift of the Father, is also the fruit of a loving and unitive relationship between God and Mary—and ultimately between God and humanity.

Mary's maternity is cloaked in the fatherhood of God. The presence of Christ Jesus within her womb was a silent testimony of the presence of his divine Father. Jesus proceeded as fruit from the nature of each of them: from God came his divinity and from Mary his humanity. His incarnation flowed from the meeting of heaven and earth in love. Heaven and earth are brought together, distinct but inseparable, in the person of Jesus Christ.

The birth of Jesus teaches us that God does not act alone not because he *can't,* but because he *won't*. If Jesus himself came into our world by the action of both God and the Virgin Mary, we ought to conclude that his life within us depends both on God and on us. We cannot be his disciples any other way. God takes the initiative when giving us life in the womb and when giving us life in faith and baptism. But we are not spectators in our spiritual lives. Although we cannot create or live the life of faith alone, it is not God's plan that we be only receivers, but also co-creators.

Divine life, like human life, blossoms within us as the fruit of a loving and unitive relationship. If we make the mistake of thinking that we ourselves can produce such fruit, or that God will present it in our lives gift-wrapped and without our participation, we will be sorely disappointed. Either we will become exhausted in the attempt or unimpressed by the results.

If we want the life of Christ to grow in our lives we must, like Mary, be overshadowed by the power of the Holy Spirit. Faith is a gift. But the *life of faith* is the fruit of our communion with God in the context of our communion with one another. Our deepest hunger is for love, joy, peace, patience, kindness, goodness, faithfulness, gentleness, and self-control (cf. Gal 5:22). These fruits of the Holy Spirit are not something we can achieve ourselves. They must be *fathered* in our hearts by the Spirit.

I thank you, Father, that you are at work in my life; that you are not a distant spectator, but alive and active in all I do. Lord, there is nothing I have and nothing I am that doesn't come from you. Without you, Lord, there is nothing at all.

But sometimes, Father, I act as if my life is mine alone and that even my faith comes from me. Trying to live my life for you, I often neglect to live it with you. Seeking to produce fruit on my own, I forget to seek the union with you from which all good fruit comes. And when I'm exhausted by it all, I wonder why you don't just give me perfect faith wrapped up with a bow.

Lord, keep me from becoming a spectator in my own inner life. When I want only to receive, show me how to give. Keep me also from trying to become the master of my own soul. Remind me that your shadow is brighter than my light. Overshadow my heart with your Holy Spirit that your fruit would be conceived in my life. Then, protect what your right hand has planted in my soul, O God, and be the eternal Father of my faith. Amen.

Chapter 8

A Family Matter

Discovering whose we are

...I bow my knees before the Father, from whom every family in heaven and on earth takes its name.

Ephesians 4:9

One weekend morning, as I lay in bed struggling to find the motivation to begin another day, our oldest daughter entered the room. She was six at the time and very excited about expecting a new baby. She sat down on the bed and told me that she had been thinking (usually a dangerous thing for a six-year-old!). Then she came out with it. When the new baby came, she said calmly, she could kind of be its mother.

As cute as our little girl was, I did inform her that she could not be the new baby's mother. *I* was the baby's only mother, and hers, too, even if she had momentarily forgotten that. She left our room looking rather sad.

As soon as those words left my lips, I knew how wrong they were. Of course my baby was mine, but not mine *alone*. Each child born to us was my husband's and mine, but not *only* ours. Our children were sons or daughters, but they were brothers, sisters, grandchildren, nieces, and nephews, too. All my little girl was trying to establish was that our new baby would somehow belong to her. She was right.

There is no greater joy than what we can experience as part of a loving family. In family we find our identity and the security of belonging. We respond to the challenges that flow from encounters with each other. We grow in love by yielding to one another. We rejoice in the sheer variety of life as we discover in others the talents we ourselves do not possess. Finally, we find the wonderful satisfaction of working together as part of living something greater than just ourselves.

No new baby enters the world in a vacuum. With every child comes a whole set of relationships. As our family has grown, I have become more and more aware that our children don't just belong to my husband and me, but to our family as a whole. We are not just parents and children, but brothers and sisters as well. Each of us belongs to all the rest.

If Mary had ever made the mistake of thinking that Jesus was only her child, or only hers and God's, it couldn't have lasted very long. Right from the start the circle was ever expanding. Unless Joseph had been willing to accept Mary's child as his own, Jesus may not have been born. Within hours of his birth, shepherds arrived at the stable to claim him. Within days, Simeon prophesied that he would be the salvation of Israel. And within months, Gentile sages worshipped him as one belonging to all the world. Jesus entered history as the "glory to [his] people Israel" (Lk 2:32) and as "a light to the nations" (Is 42:6).

The Christ we worship is both the Son of God and the Son of Mary. He is fully hers and fully God's. But we worship Jesus because he is *ours*. He entered our world not simply as the Son of God and of Mary, but as "the firstborn within a large family" (Rm 8:29). Each of us can claim him as our own, because he came not just as part of the Holy Family, but to establish the eternal family of faith.

Jesus brought with him a web of relationships in both blood and Spirit. When we are his, we become part of that network of relations. We are born—and reborn—into a family. In the Spirit we are not only God's children, but brothers and sisters to one another in Christ.

God places us and our lives of faith in families not just because they are necessary or useful, but because they are the ideal. A family is more than the sum of its members. So too, the Church is much greater than the aggregate of individuals sitting in the pews. We are each empowered to become more than what we are—more that what any of us could be alone—simply by accepting one another as our own in the same way that we accept Christ. Out of the unity and diversity that every family is, God makes us the Body of Christ.

Like any family, the Church has its problems. We are not always there for one another. We sometimes squabble over how we think things ought to be done or who should be doing them. We struggle to put up with one another, let alone love each other. At times, we hurt each other deeply due to our infirmities and, sadly, our infidelities. But no matter how very difficult or dysfunctional family life can be, the life of faith is a family life.

Our claims to be the children of God are predicated on our belonging to the *family* of God. The measure of our belonging to God is reflected in the measure of our belonging to one another. If God is our Father, we will have many brothers and sisters. There are no "only children" in the heavenly household.

We cannot live the fullness of faith in a vacuum. Deep discipleship blossoms in a garden of many flowers. The Father gathers us to himself like an eternal bouquet. The beauty of a single blossom is not diminished by the crowd. Rather, each one in its place is enhanced by those around it.

Lord God, I thank you for calling me to yourself and for making me your own. I praise you for being not only a Father to me, but a Brother, and a Spouse as well. But Lord, when I rejoice that you are mine, I sometimes forget that there are others too. At times I want to keep you to myself, for myself, and pretend that you have called me and me alone.

Lord, remind me that your arms embrace the world and that in your eternal family there are many children. Help me to accept all your children as my true brothers and sisters. Give me the grace to forgive those who have hurt me and to ask the forgiveness of those whom I have hurt. Teach me to value your call in others' lives. And help me to glorify you in union with all who call you Father. Amen.

Chapter 9

Where Do Babies Come From?

Preparing and including your other children

I came that they may have life, and have it abundantly.

John 10:10

Life is full of mystery, and so is the woman who is full of life. If we stop long enough to fully consider how all this birthing business really works, we have to admit that the whole account reads more like science fiction or fairy tale than reality. Even when we are going through it ourselves, there's no getting around the fact that the process is odd. Even if we think we know it all, even if we've been through it before, we invariably have questions as we find ourselves in previously uncharted waters. Pregnancies can be as distinct as the children who emerge from them. And, too, we ourselves change. Because we grow and develop, we do not experience the same things in the same way.

If pregnancy astonishes us, it amazes children even more. Some children are very observant, noticing—and commenting on—just about every pound gained. Others are quite oblivious, unaware of even the most drastic changes occurring right in front of them. When a small child thinks about the baby who is in "mommy's tummy," a whole line of precious reasoning develops. Children desperately need to make sense of what is going on in pregnancy. For instance, when our second daughter was five years old, she burst into tears when she happened to catch me in a bout of morning sickness. She was afraid that I would throw up her new brother or sister along with my breakfast!

A pregnant woman in the house also gives rise to the question: "Where do babies come from?" Children do need answers to this question, but not necessarily all the answers. I think adults often think a child is asking for more information than he or she really wants or needs. This question is more often than not an exploration of that child's own identity and origins. It is less frequently a request for a lesson in anatomy. Children want and need to know that they were created by God, loved into existence, and wanted. They also need to know that everyone arrives on earth in pretty much the same way and in pretty much the same state.

As oldest children get older, however, I think they can hear and accept some of the deeper truths of human love and life. I have found that including older children right from the onset of pregnancy provided the best opportunity for them to grow in their love and acceptance of a new baby in the house. Going to obstetrician visits, feeling the baby move, seeing ultrasound images, and constantly hashing out names: these things make it possible for children to take a part in the great adventure of expanding family life.

We've tried to teach our children that love and life are as inseparable from each other as they are from responsibility. I got a bit daring with the birth of our sixth child and asked our two oldest girls if they might be interested in attending the delivery. Then ten and twelve years old, they jumped at the chance. While they did choose to look away at times, the experience definitely gave them more reverence for life as well as a greater sense of God as the source of life. It did so for them in much the same way it does for any of us: simply by being there, watching and waiting and wondering at it all. Three years later, they were back in the delivery room again for the birth of our youngest child.

Having our daughters attend childbirth helped to bridge the considerable age gap between our oldest and youngest children. The time they will have together under our roof is, regrettably, very brief. The oldest two will have left home before their littlest sister is in kindergarten. But their presence at those two births has enabled them to form a deeper relationship with their younger siblings than they may have had otherwise. And as they were becoming young women themselves, it strengthened my relationship with them, too.

The most important thing to realize is that our children may not feel the way we do about a pregnancy. We can be overwhelmed while an older child is enthusiastic and excited. Conversely, we can feel like our prayers have been answered while a child can feel threatened, afraid, or ambivalent. Children in the same family don't necessarily feel the same way about a new baby either. Preferences can loom very large at times. Often it has a lot to do with the "color" of the expected bundle: pink or blue. While some children look forward to playing mommy with what they perceive to be a very lifelike new doll, others can be apprehensive about how another birth will change their place in the family.

The key to welcoming a new member of the family is sensitivity. Older children must know concretely that they are loved, that they will continue to be important to us, and that we will care for their needs even if and when a new baby arrives. Talking with children openly about their feelings, thoughts, and expectations is a good way to begin. But those conversations ought to be complemented with an honest assessment of our own feelings, thoughts, and expectations. Most mothers hope for a "tightly-knit" family. But not all loving families will fit into that mold. Some brothers and sisters will be close all their lives. Others simply won't.

Borrowing a strategy from my husband's aunt, I always told the youngest child at the time that the new baby would be his or her "special baby." I made sure that the youngest was first at hospital visits and opportunities to hold the newborn. I told her that she would be the one who was the most important helper and guardian—throughout life, that younger child would look to her first. With eight children, this simple technique has created a domino effect of loving concern between children. Not that the "next one down" isn't also the most annoying child to the one who is just ahead. But all our children have responded to that call to care just a little more intently for their "special" babies.

Mary never had to prepare other children to welcome the baby Jesus as a younger sibling. Nor did she have to prepare Jesus to be another child's older brother. Yet, in a mysterious way, Mary is a mother to us all, and Jesus is our brother. The arms of the Father, longing to welcome every daughter and son, are stretched out in the arms of Jesus reaching for his mother Mary. Those same arms embrace the world from the cross. We are indeed brothers and sisters to each other in Christ, even when we do not recognize each other as such.

Our identity as the family of God is expressed in many ways. We are each a "special baby" to our baptismal godparents or confirmation sponsors. In professing one faith and one baptism, we share a common identity. We are brought to unity around one holy table. We find in each other spiritual fathers and mothers who nurture our lives of discipleship, and many brothers and sisters with whom we grow toward maturity. It is easier to see God in some than in others; but we are called to acknowledge the Divine Presence in all persons we encounter.

The Church is the ever-expanding family of God. Through baptism, newborn disciples are welcomed every day. Some of them are younger in faith than we are. Others have traveled further along the road of the cross than we have. As in any family, sometimes we are loving and close; however, in other ways, we may be distant or competitive. Response is always a choice. We can discover the fullness of who we are in the context of our relationships. Or we can feel threatened and unsure in what can seem like a crowd of strangers.

Through Christ we are all related as daughters and sons of the same Heavenly Father, conceived and sustained by his love. Gathered around the eternal banquet table, many of us will hardly believe our eyes. Our eternal family will encompass every kind of person and personality, every culture and language, age and time. It is for that feast that we live to prepare our hearts—the feast where all are welcome, because all are family.

O Lord, I am blessed to be the venue of your creativity. I am astonished at how you continue to bring forth new life. No one can outdo you in generosity. Again and again you love me in new ways. Yet sometimes, Lord, I'm not sure how I feel. And sometimes I'm afraid of what others may think. I am not always aware of your hand in my life. I don't always see your work in the lives of others.

Help me to be ready for every gift you want to give. But Lord, help me to prepare others too, for all you will do for them and through them. Show me the breadth of your love in all of us, and teach me to prepare your way. Amen.

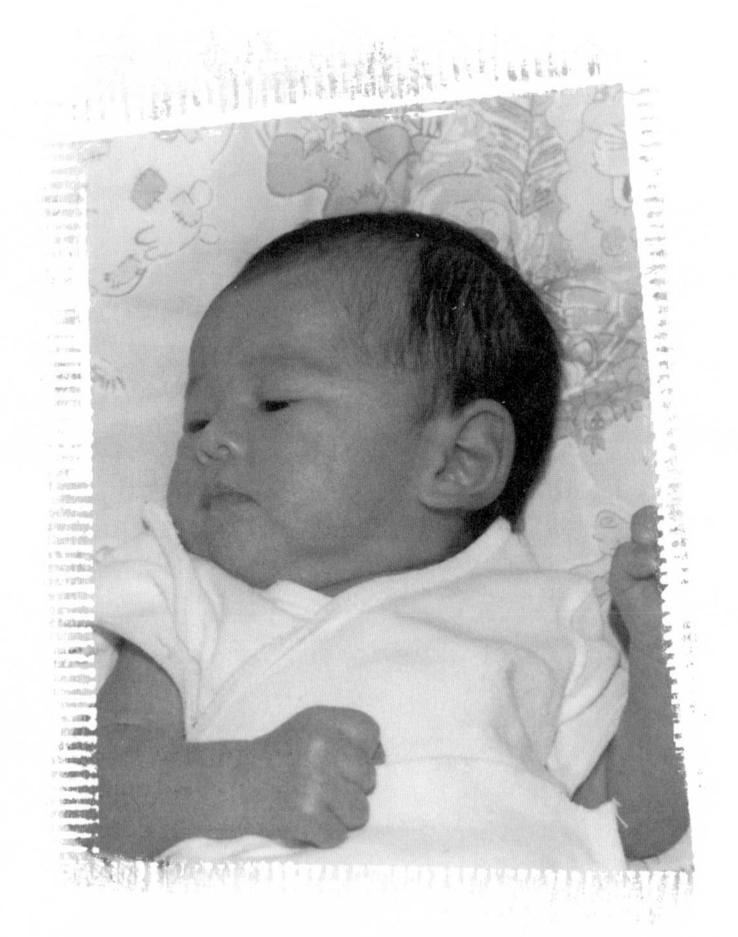

Chapter 10

The Solo Act

The challenges of single-mothering

> He will feed his flock like a shepherd; he will gather the lambs in his arms, and carry them in his bosom, and gently lead the mother sheep.
>
> Isaiah 40:11

Did you ever notice how, just when you finally catch up with yourself, everything goes haywire all at once? It is as if the scientific laws of the universe included a strange and seemingly unrelated chain reaction of cause and effect. There is a quiet moment, so the telephone rings. You have a little extra money, so suddenly your car breaks down. I'm convinced that the most effective way to wake a sleeping baby is to sit down with a cup of tea, and the best guarantee that your children will need go to the bathroom is to get them into the car. Life rarely goes smoothly or as planned. It's no wonder mothers can be a bit paranoid!

Sometimes even minor snags or inconveniences have an enormous ripple effect. It's a challenge for anyone just to keep up with it all, but for the single mother, the challenges are even greater. The "traditional" family has a certain built-in back up system simply because there are an extra pair of adult hands regularly involved. But there are instances in which every family has to reach beyond itself and enlist someone else's help.

When I was pregnant with our oldest son, the reality of my dependence—not only my husband, but on my entire family—became crystal clear. By the time I was four months along, my doctor alerted me to the possibility that I might be carrying twins. I was so huge by six months that everyone I encountered thought I was overdue. I remember going shopping and being amazed as the sea of people divided in front of me.

Any cause I might have had for believing myself entirely self-sufficient vanished during that pregnancy. I was perpetually exhausted, had difficulty moving around, and was in constant pain. I had to rely on the people around me to take over many of the things that I had done for myself and for them. I needed help to clean, to care for the two children I already had, and even putting on socks and shoes. I often wondered what I would have done without the loving people in my life.

Experiencing such challenges myself, I can only imagine how much more difficult pregnancy must be for the single mother. The truth is that just as it takes more than one person to conceive new life, it takes more than one to sustain it. All of us are dependent on one another at various times in our lives. We are created needing God and each other.

There are times when every mother feels alone. Being a single mother only intensifies those feelings. Thankfully, however, no woman really has to raise her children all alone. I say "thankfully," because no woman really can. The single mother, however, may have to search farther afield to find the resources and assistance she needs. There is a great deal of help for mothers out there, and many people who are happy to celebrate new life with all of them. It may take a while to track down, but if the solo mother searches for support she will find it. It just may not be where she had expected it.

It takes deep personal courage to raise a child or children by yourself. All single mothers should be applauded for their determination and love. Choosing to give life is choosing to honor the Giver of life. With God all things are possible. The single mother can travel the road ahead of her with grace and confidence in the Lord. Taking one step at a time, she can find her way through the challenges. She can rise to the occasion and inspire others to overcome the obstacles they will face in life.

If we look, we may see in the eyes of every single mother a reflection of Mary. Often we focus so much on Mary's holiness that we fail to see her as those around her would have. It is hard for some of us to accept that Mary's friends probably saw her as an unwed mother. Who would have believed a story like hers? I don't think I would have. Perhaps she didn't even bother to tell it.

Mary trusted God not only with her body, but with her reputation and with her life. When she consented to bear the Son of God, Mary had no guarantees. She suspected that there would be no angels to answer the questions that others would ask. She knew, too, that both her marriage and her life could be in jeopardy. Perhaps trusting God may have begun to look rather easy when she realized that she'd have to trust her friends and family and Joseph as well. What of all the talk, the rejection, the dishonor that was in store? Was this the "blessedness" the angel said would be hers?

But God did not abandon Mary to the law, her parents' disbelief, Joseph's doubts, or even village gossip. In giving his Son to the world, God's promise of salvation to all of us was not fulfilled at Mary's expense. Rather, God provided her with the support she needed not only to endure the circumstances of her pregnancy, but also to find joy in it.

This support was not extraordinary or mystical. It was the same kind of support that is available to us all. That is, the care of other people who love us. Mary found God's providence in Joseph, in her cousin Elizabeth, and in the stranger who offered her a warm stable on a cold night. Through other people, both near and far, God provided for the holy family. The rich gifts of the wise men were not meant to be put in a curio cabinet. The gold, frankincense, and myrrh probably kept them afloat as they fled for their lives into Egypt. God still provides for mothers and their children today. Families, churches, schools at every level, medical professionals, organizations, and social service agencies can and do help make solo mothering not only possible, but joyous and successful.

A crisis pregnancy, whether we are personally involved in it or not, may grieve and disappoint us. It can make us feel disillusioned with each other or tempt us to become cynical toward things we can't control. But it also presents us with an opportunity to love the way God does—unconditionally. We learn unconditional love when we find ourselves surrounded by conditions that we would not have chosen ourselves; we practice it when we find a way to accept the unexpected in ourselves and others.

God saw not only to Mary's material needs, but also to those that were emotional and spiritual. God's call to the Church is that we not abandon one another, but rather fulfill his law by bearing one another's burdens. God cares for *all* mothers as much as he did Mary. *All* life is miraculous, and *all* children are God's children.

Lord, I thank you for all the people you have placed in my life—those who are there for me, and those for whom I am there. I praise you, God, for weaving us inextricably into each other's lives. You have shown us that it is love, and not weakness, that makes us dependent on one another and on you. Lord, when I am tired and have lost my strength I often feel so alone. Sometimes it seems as if everyone has turned away. At times, I wonder if even you have abandoned me.

Help me, Lord, to know the strength of your love surrounding me. Teach me that because you are with me, there is nothing I have to bear alone. Give me the grace to ask for help when I need it. And when someone asks my help, give me a heart that will not turn away. Amen.

Chapter 11

You Are Not Alone

The mystery of being with

"I am with you always, to the end of the age."
Matthew 28:20

"Pregnant" used to be an unwelcome word even when it was a welcome event. Until not long ago, our manners demanded that we use other, more delicate ways of conveying the news that someone was going to have a baby. We invented all kinds of euphemisms to cloak our squeamishness about such matters. There were ways of talking about "it" without having to say anything about "her." Remember the stork, the pumpkin patch, and the doctor? So-and-so was never "pregnant," she was "expecting." (I remember as a little girl wondering just *what* she was expecting. I thought it might be something like a package from UPS!)

When we talk about pregnancy, many of us still prefer to choose our words from this more "genteel"

vocabulary menu. I find something uncomfortable in describing myself or someone else as "pregnant." For me, it's not because pregnancy is scandalous in some way, but because the word itself falls far short of the whole reality as I experience it. It focuses on the physiological alone. It is invasive in communicating the physical details, yet evasive of the emotional and spiritual aspects of maternity.

Antique and out of fashion as it is, I think the best way of describing pregnancy is the phrase "with child." In truth, *presence* is what pregnancy is all about. No matter what she faces, from the moment of conception a pregnant woman does not face it alone. She is constantly with someone else physically, of course, but emotionally and spiritually as well. The very nature of pregnancy requires a woman to be in the continual presence of the child (or children!) she carries. She is always *with child.*

The pregnant woman is full or, rather, filled with life—not just her own, but her child's also. She is quietly occupied with the secret someone who is not only with her, but *within* her. Every mother is abundant with interpersonal activity. She and her child are alive to one another at every level of being.

At times this abundance overflows into bursts of energy. I remember stenciling a bedroom wall, cleaning absolutely everything, painting a few closets and bookcases, moving furniture, and even squeezing (and I mean squeezing!) between bushes to stain the front steps while pregnant. With much less fondness, I also recall fits of rage, uncontrollable tears, and emotional roller coasters that always seemed to be speeding downhill.

Sadly, it is easy for the spiritual abundance of pregnancy to elude us. Perhaps we focus too much on the physical realities that stare us in the face and on the urgencies thrust upon us by emotional currents. We know in our hearts that there is something more, something deeply *spiritual* to maternity. But somehow it seems difficult to find and lay hold of that intimate spiritual significance for more than fleeting moments. What is urgent so easily distracts us from what is important.

The sign that God would give to confirm the coming of the Messiah was that a virgin would conceive and bear a son; that his name would be called Emmanuel, "God-is-with-us." When the angel first appeared to Mary, his greeting to her might have seemed a bit strange. It is the greeting we recall with familiarity when we pray the Hail Mary. The angel recognizes the presence of the Holy Spirit in Mary's soul: "Full of grace," he says, "the Lord is with you" (cf. Lk 1:28).

Mary indeed was full of grace. She blossomed like a flower for whom the entire garden was cultivated; like a plant that had never been outside the greenhouse of God's intimate presence. She had been caught up into the divine love of the Trinity. The fullness of her grace flowed from that same communion of divine love.

In some respects, becoming the mother of the Savior did not change Mary's relationship with God at all. Even before her assent to the will of God in her own life, the angel had called her "full of grace." Even before she actually conceived, he had already told her "the Lord is with you."

And yet, for Mary, as for every one of us, bearing a child must have been a watershed event. When Mary was with child, she was in the physical presence of the Lord who had always been with her spiritually. Pregnancy enabled Mary to experience being with God continually, just as we are all in the perpetual presence of our unborn children. I cannot begin to imagine the God who created all the heavens and the earth being physically *within* me. Can you?

But in a wonderfully mystical way—through faith and baptism—we no longer have to imagine that God *is* with us, or even *within* us. The presence of God is as close and as real as the presence of our unborn children in the womb. We see this in the Scriptures that tell us that it is "in him we live and move and have our being" (Acts 17:28). God is the world in which our spirits live and grow.

We are filled with grace from the very same God who filled the heart of Mary. Grace confined Jesus to the womb of Mary just as our children are held captive for a time within our bodies. It is that grace which confines the awesome divine presence *within* our hearts and lives. It may have been enough for us to have God with us, but it was not enough for God. God's thirst for intimacy could not be quenched by simply being *with*—he had to be *within*.

Our Lord's greatest desire is that we become as present to him as he is to us; that we not only be with God, but within God. Presence has always been the promise and the purpose of the divine plan. There is not a moment of our lives when God is absent. God does not—and will not—abandon us. We can live our lives with confidence, knowing that we are never truly alone. Whatever paths we walk, and whether we walk them willingly or not, we are always with God because the Holy One is within us. Our God is Emmanuel not only for Mary, but also for us and all the world.

Lord, you have shown me that from the moment my life began, I have never been alone. Because I am part of the pulse of life, my whole being teems with the activity that surrounds me.

Although my life is lived in the context of your presence and in the continual presence of others, I can still become preoccupied with myself. Sometimes I rush along emotional currents too quickly to sense the significance of another's presence. I grasp my own experience without understanding that the life that surrounds me—and that moves within me—is not simply my own.

Lord, teach me to be attentive to others. Empty me of myself when I begin to overflow, and fill me instead with an awareness of your presence. Quench your thirst for intimacy with my soul. In the midst of all my frantic activity, give me peace. Make my heart your temple and my life a place where all I meet may encounter you. Amen.

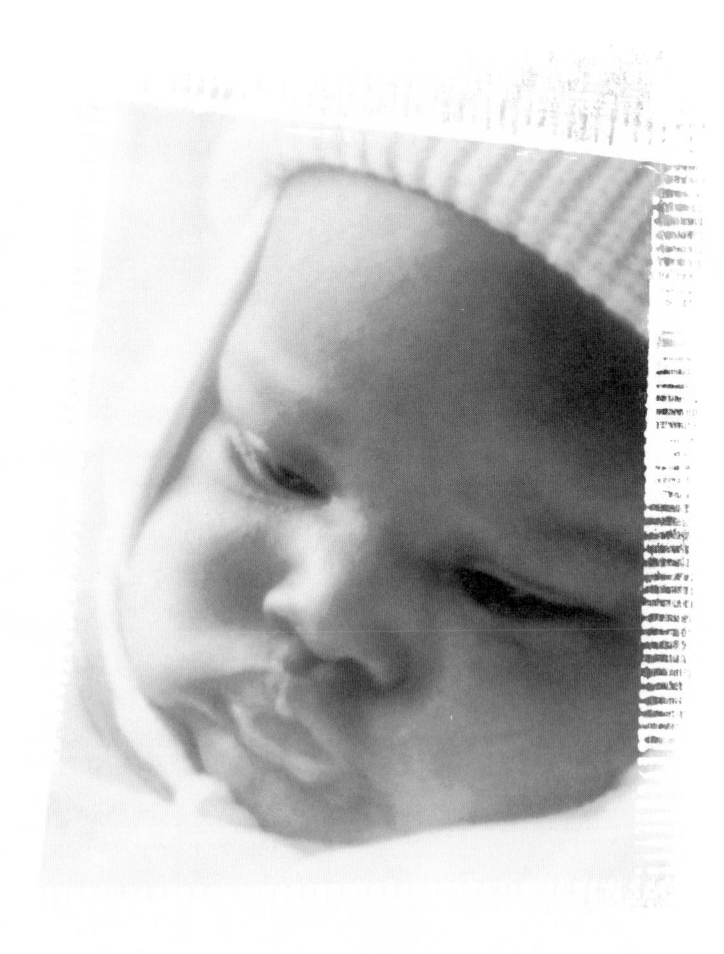

Chapter 12

You Are Never Alone, Not Even When You *Want* to Be!

Dealing with the job that never ends

Where can I go from your spirit?
Or where can I flee from your presence?
Psalm 139:7

How comforting it is to know that we are never truly alone—and how aggravating it is when we *want* to be alone! I have found that I have limits to how long I can stand being around people, even those I love. There is something inside me that craves solitude, that enjoys being alone. Many have experienced the breakup of good friendships simply because of what I like to call "overdose." There does seem to be such a thing as being together too much.

Before our third child was a year old, my husband lost his job. The economy wasn't very strong at the time, and although he was qualified for many positions, there just weren't many openings. Because he was able to get a few independent contracts, we decided that he would try building a business of his own. In the absence of other choices, he set up shop in a corner of our bedroom. Although he spent more and more hours isolated behind that bedroom door, I felt his continual presence cramping my style. Just knowing he was there began to grate on me. I kept wishing he would just *get out of my house!* Similarly, when the nine of us finally moved out of our six room house, we realized just how many of our little arguments arose simply because we were constantly in each other's way.

But if absence really does make the heart grow fonder, what of the woman who is inescapably with child? There is no way a pregnant woman can distance herself from her baby—at least not physically. There is nothing she can do to get some space. There are no boundaries that can be drawn between them. They are always together. They are never alone. And although the depth and joy of pregnancy is rooted in this intimacy, it is precisely this intimacy that can really begin to get on our nerves.

Even before her baby is born a mother is on-call. Her body is at her child's disposal. A first-time mother learns quickly that maternity is more than a full-time job. The business of having a family is very much like a family business. It is a venture with convenience store hours—and it's not her convenience that comes first.

As wonderful as it is to be with child, there are times that all of us would like very much to be alone. Growing up as an only child, I think that I have been particularly sensitive to this loss of solitude, especially between the hours of eleven at night and seven in the morning! I have seen my children struggle with this too. As much as they love each new baby that comes home, they can really get tired of having to change their plans and patterns to accommodate the little bundle. Toddlers, they have each discovered in turn, are expert wrecking crew material.

Maternity pushes us to all our limits, and beyond. Not only our physical energy, but our emotional resources can be easily spent. There is no human state that is more demanding or consuming. Sometimes I have imagined myself wearing an "Occupied" sign around my neck. I have often wondered how I might trade it in for a "Do Not Disturb!"

Our lives of faith are not unlike pregnancy in these respects. There have certainly been times in which I have grown tired of feeling God breathe down the back of my neck; times when I have wished the "Hound of Heaven" would bark up some other tree. I am never completely sure how to respond. The strangeness, mystery, and novelty of the divine presence is undeniably attractive. But the depth of intimacy that God pursues is often annoying and unnerving.

Many of us spend our whole lives caught in this dilemma. While we want what we need from God, we run from what can seem like the endless demands of God in our lives. We want our Lord to be close enough to hear and answer us; but few of us allow God to come as close to us as he desires. When the Almighty draws just a little too near, we can find ourselves searching everywhere for a place to hide. We throw up our hands when we find that there is none.

I can imagine Mary experiencing this. From the very little we know about her life, it may have seemed to Mary as if things would never be quiet again. As soon as one thing was resolved, three others took its place.

She consents to conceive the Son of God only to find herself at a loss to explain it all to Joseph. An angel appears and Joseph's doubts disappear, but then they are required to travel to Bethlehem. When they arrive, there is no room for them—except in a cave. The baby is born, but the moments just after birth are interrupted by a ragged band of shepherds, almost indistinguishable from their sheep—at least in terms of odor. When the infant Jesus is presented at the Temple as prescribed by Jewish law, the prophet Simeon proclaims that he is the Savior. But his word to Mary about the sword that was to pierce her heart casts a shadow on the joy. Finally, just as everything seems to calm down, wise men arrive. The good news is that they brought gifts; the bad news is that Herod wants to kill the child and they must then flee to Egypt.

This whirlwind is what we celebrate as the "Joyful Mysteries" of the Rosary. We often say that when it rains, it pours. Mary must have felt as if she had been caught in the great flood.

Mary could have chosen to try to flee from God, just as she and Joseph had fled from Herod's wrath. Instead, Mary lived by faith. She did not abandon the One who would not abandon her. Instead of running away from God's presence, she ran toward it. Instead of struggling against God, she conformed her life and herself to him as much as she was able. She trusted that because there was no place to hide from God, he would be her hiding place from all that makes life difficult.

I have come to the conclusion that shaking your fist at the inevitable is even more exhausting than accepting it. There is a certain interior peace that comes when—and only when—we surrender to the limitations of our lives. We all have limitations. In a certain sense they help define us. But all the interruptions, the noise, the commotion, and even our own frustrations—these things are external to mothering. They are merely skin-deep. They need not contribute to an inner desperation. Maternity is much deeper than that. A mother I am, and a mother I will be. It is not what I *do*; it is bound up with who I *am*.

When we are overwhelmed by the responsibilities of motherhood, it may help to remember that our children's very lives depend on our presence. Likewise, when we tire of God's presence in our lives, when we want to be left alone, it may do us good to remember that we were created for the purpose of being with God not only for a moment, but for all eternity. We are attached to the Lord forever by the umbilical cord of our faith and baptism. We are as dependent upon God as the unborn children we carry are upon us—even more so.

Lord, as grateful as I am to have you near, I have to admit that there are times I wish you would leave me alone. At those times, O God, your invitations sound like demands, your breath feels like a hurricane, and your touch irritates more than it comforts.

I have tried all the escape routes I could find, but no matter where I've run or turned, you have always been there waiting. Afraid of what going deeper might mean, I have exhausted myself contending with you. My arms have grown weary from pushing you away.

Lord, help me to remember that without you there is nothing, and that beyond you there is only darkness. When I grow resentful of my dependence on you, teach me to be grateful for all you have done for me. When I try to run away, run after me, Lord. Catch me in your arms, and carry me into eternity with you. Amen.

Chapter 13

Caregiving and Care Taking

You have needs too!

"Your Father knows what you need before you ask him."

Matthew 6:8

"It is more blessed to give than to receive." As true as that statement is, there's no getting around the fact that we are all receivers as well as givers—we have to be. While we may spend a great deal of our lives taking care of other people, our own needs don't simply disappear.

When we're expecting a baby, we are more keenly aware of our needs than we are otherwise. We don't really have different needs than we normally do, but in some ways they are deeper. We are hungrier, more tired, more in need of personal connectedness. All of that is because, whether we feel it or not, we are giving constant care to that little someone else inside us.

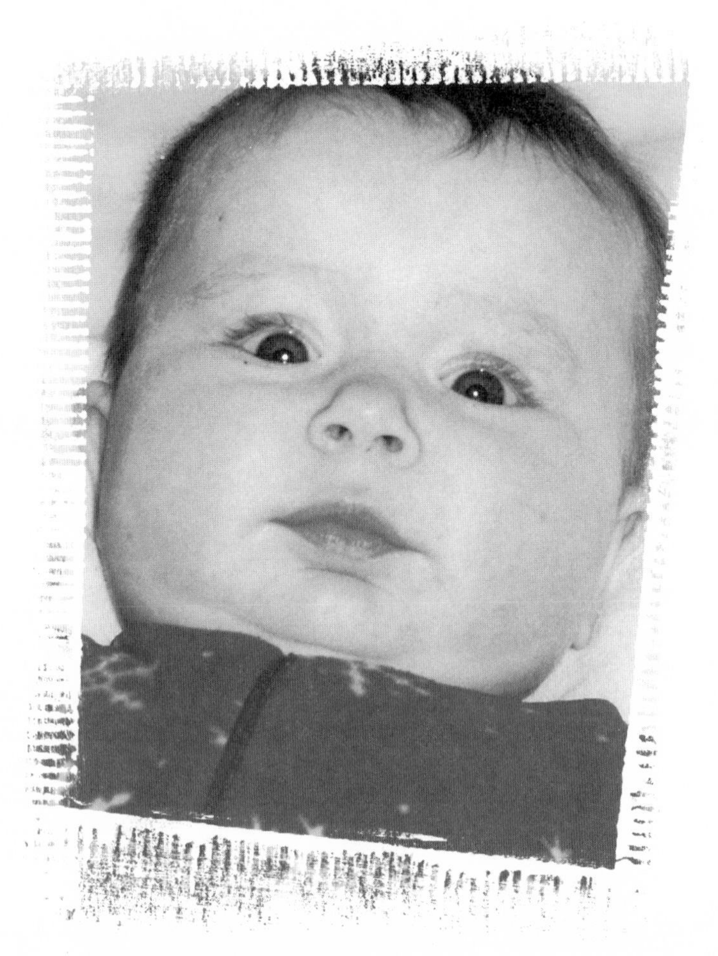

Most women don't seem to have a problem with self-care during a pregnancy. The prenatal medical appointments—the ones that make you feel like you live in the doctor's office—keep a mother's needs on the radar screen. Not long after the child is born, however, a lot of us get so involved in caregiving that we forget to take care of ourselves. Our own needs drop out of view. Partly, I think, this is because many women think that they are expected to do "it" all. In the long run, just about everything falls into the "it" category: excellent meals, immaculate housekeeping, impeccable personal appearance, a promising career, and brilliant, well-behaved children. When we can't do "it" all, something—often a moment of self-care—gets eliminated.

I remember walking through a mall once with our first two children in a double stroller. Catching a glimpse of myself in the window glass, I was appalled at what I saw. I looked terrible. My hair was a mess, my clothes were grungy, and my overall appearance shouted "low self-esteem." The truth was I didn't have a low self-image. But with all the care I had to give to my children, I had stopped caring for myself. Then and there I set a different standard, went home, and changed my clothes.

It is tempting to think that the best mothers are women who care so completely for their children that they have stopped caring at all about themselves. In reality, we need to find a balance between the care we give and the care we need to take. Perhaps selflessness has something to do with caring less *about* ourselves. But it is not selfish to care *for* ourselves. Self-care isn't the same as self-indulgence.

The distinction between caring *for* and caring *about* is easier to grasp when we realize that it can be difficult to tell the difference between needs and wants. Health, for example, is a need. Bodybuilding would be a desire (for someone other than myself!). Unfortunately, the line between needs and wants isn't always that clear. Our desires can be rather fuzzy. Stress makes things even fuzzier.

Genuine needs are rarely demanding. When I feel dissatisfied and start running around in circles, I begin to suspect that I may have some unmet need lying just beneath the surface. Most needs can be addressed rather easily. Often we don't even have to walk out the door to recharge our batteries; we just have to find the nearest power outlet. Sometimes that is as simple as a few extra moments in the bathroom or a bottle of vitamins. Over the years, I've discovered ways of providing for my own needs—and many of my wants—within the framework of my family responsibilities. I've learned to search out those things in my life that give me life, like taking a class or a nap, and to balance them against those things that drain me, like doing laundry.

Every human being has a share of both wants and needs. When we look at our own or others' needs, we ought to resist thinking of wants as somehow intrinsically selfish or needs as non-negotiable. Over the years I have had to periodically recalibrate myself by identifying desires appropriately. But even more, I have had to learn to discern whether I can or should put one of my needs or wants on the sidelines in favor of somebody else's. Family life presents countless opportunities for heroic generosity and self-sacrifice. Our holiness increases when we respond to some of them; but if we take advantage of all of them, we are likely to burn ourselves out.

In caring for others, we participate in God's care for every human being as the bearer of his image. Still, we need to care for the divine image in us as well. Caregiving can tap us out. It can push us to our limits and beyond. While living for others is a noble goal, somewhere along the line we must come to the realization that God does not ask us to do more than we are able. Rather, the Lord teaches us that we cannot truly meet the needs of others without also addressing our own.

At the root, all of us are needy in pretty much the same way. Each of us needs to love and to be loved, and we cannot meet this deepest need ourselves. The need to love and be loved can only be met by God and other people. Love gives us life to begin with, and love continues to be life-giving. The family is the prime setting for making love concrete in both directions—giving and receiving. The home is meant to be the place where the language of love is continually spoken. There are times when I will be the subject of love's dialogue, and times when I will be its object.

Mary cared for her family without the help of a washer and dryer, disposable diapers, or even an oven. Her days were longer and harder than ours in many respects; but there was a simplicity in her life that gave clarity to her own needs and the needs of others. Without all the exterior noise of a very busy world, perhaps it was less difficult to avoid being distracted from what is truly important and not just urgent or attractive. Neither Mary's life nor her heart were cluttered with unnecessary things. Her days were filled with attending to the most basic needs she and her family shared—the material, social, and spiritual staples of human existence.

The simplicity of Mary's life paints a picture of what it means to be "poor in spirit" (Mt 5:3). Such poverty is simply the recognition that we need God's presence in our hearts and lives. Mary's greatest wisdom, perhaps, was the awareness of her own need for God. Although she was the servant of the Lord, Mary did not find any reason to deny that she needed to be served as well. She was not ashamed of or guilty about her needs. Not wrapping herself in a pretense of self-sufficiency, Mary received all the great things the Almighty did for her with gratitude and joy.

I can imagine there were times when Mary felt overwhelmed or exhausted by the daily grind just as we do. Certainly, she looked to Joseph and later to her Son, Jesus, and then the apostle John, for the care she herself needed. And while we do not really know what her specific personal needs were, undoubtedly God and those who loved her did. What we do know is that she shared with us the most basic human need for love. God is that Love. Mary's deepest need was—and ours is—for God.

O God, you know my needs better than I do, and you see each one of them as an opportunity to love me. You never grow tired of caring for me.

Sometimes though, Lord, in caring for others, I act as if I don't have needs of my own. Instead of simply doing what you've asked of me, I undertake the impossible.

Lord, help me to serve those who are closest to me; but give me the ability to take the care that I myself need. Keep me from both resentment and self-indulgence. Guard me from denying my own limitations and needs. And help me to find both strength and fulfillment in you. Amen.

Chapter 14

Becoming a Dwelling

Our changing bodies

We are the temple of the living God.
2 Corinthians 6:16

Most of us are intrigued by how we look when we're expecting. We all marvel at how our bodies change shape. We study our profiles in the mirror with both shock and delight. We ask our friends and mates about how much we "show." First-time mothers may try to imagine just how far they will have to sit from the dinner table at the end. Experienced mothers catch themselves making comparisons between pregnancies. Every culture has its own formula for figuring out whether the baby is a boy or a girl simply by looking at the mother. It's amazing, but many of them really seem to work!

When I was carrying our second child, a few of our friends were expecting children as well. One morning after church, my husband observed that seeing us all together was much like going on a whale watch. Not all of us appreciated that remark. I, for one, enjoyed a good laugh.

There is something undeniably funny about how we look when we're pregnant. What I like to call the Einstein factor enters in here: size is relative. Being only five foot two inches tall has put me at a disadvantage. The babies I carry have nowhere to grow but out. To make it worse, six of the seven babies I delivered were over nine pounds at birth—(one of our boys was ten pounds, fifteen ounces, and another was a whopping eleven-eight!). I have often joked about looking like a piece of real estate, and if I took a walk on the beach, I could even be considered oceanfront property!

All joking aside, there is some truth to the notion that maternity doesn't just make us *look* like a house, it actually turns us into one. While we are pregnant, our bodies are our baby's home. *We* are where they live.

It is a warm and welcoming spirit that makes a house a home. Likewise, it is this same kind of warmth that transforms not only our bodies, but our lives, into a "home" for all our children. Fewer and fewer of us list our occupation as "homemaker." Yet, in a real sense, that is what every mother is called to be. The physical nature of maternity gives us no choice. Our unborn babies inhabit our bodies whether we like it or not.

But emotionally and spiritually, *we* do the choosing. We all become houses, but we must *choose* to become homes. We must prepare our hearts to receive our children as diligently as we prepare our homes to receive a guest. We can clear away the clutter and disorder in our lives so that we can be as attentive to the needs of our children as we ought to be. We can choose to put our whole selves completely at their disposal or to be less than welcoming toward them with all that we are.

The Lord who made the heavens and the earth, whom all the universe cannot contain, chose to dwell in the womb of Mary. She may not have been *completely* prepared for all that being the mother of the Savior would mean. But when God came to Mary, he did not find her *un*prepared. Her heart was pure and open. Her soul was still. Her spirit was attentive and willing to submit. Mary received the Divine Guest readily.

Similarly, when Mary went to visit her cousin Elizabeth, she came as a guest to her cousin's home. Elizabeth, honored by her presence, asked, "Who am I that the mother of my Lord should come to me?" (cf. Lk 1:43) Although she had plenty of her own needs, Elizabeth placed herself at the disposal of her guest. In so doing, she welcomed into her life both Mary and the child she was carrying.

Mysteriously, even the unborn infant John welcomed Christ. He leapt for joy at the hidden presence of the divine child who made his home in the womb of Mary. He "danced" before Jesus, just as David danced before the presence of God in the Ark of the Covenant. In bearing the Son of God, we see Mary as the Ark of the *New* Covenant. She was, for a time, the home of God's salvation.

Indeed, Mary was the first person who became the dwelling place of God's presence, but she was not the last. Throughout history holy men and women have placed themselves completely at God's disposal. The Holy One wishes to make a home in *each one of us*. God first took up residence in Mary's body in order to then reside in all our hearts.

The Gospel of John tell us that "The Word became flesh, and lived among us" (Jn 1: 14)—God literally with us. Through faith it is possible for each of us to become the tent God pitches, the place in which the Lord dwells. To do so, however, we must learn and practice the art of hospitality. We must receive God in the same way that Elizabeth received Mary. Resisting any temptation to feel put out, we ought to greet God with the joy a host has at the arrival of a much longed-for guest. Our spirits can do more than just stand in the divine presence: they can learn to dance before the Lord.

It is much easier to receive a friend than it is to receive a stranger. Many of us sincerely desire intimacy with God, but we can never expect to embrace our Lord as a friend or brother or lover, unless we first welcome him as a stranger. Whoever God becomes in our lives, he appears to us first as a Divine Stranger. God approaches us as a wayfarer, as one looking for a place to dwell. Our parents may have wisely taught us to beware of strangers, but the Scriptures teach us "Do not neglect to show hospitality to strangers, for by doing that some have entertained angels without knowing it" (Heb 13:2).

Like our wombs, which stretch to become dwelling places for our unborn children, our hearts—small as they are—can become home for God. We need not be grand and glorious country mansions, we need only prepare and make room. Our lives are the poor stables in which the Lord wants to be born; our hearts the mangers in which he longs to rest; our souls the castles in which God hopes to dwell.

O Lord, all the brilliance of creation is but a candle to the splendor of your presence. You shine more gloriously than the stars; you reach above the heights of heaven, and you stand below the depths of the earth. You are so vast that not even the whole universe can contain you.

It is not on high mountains in ocean depths that you wish to dwell. You do not seek rich palaces to give you glory, but, rather, human hearts.

Lord, give me a warm and welcoming spirit. Help me to always greet you with joy. Teach me to make room for you and for others. Show me how to prepare my soul for your coming. Be born in the poor stable of my life, O God. Come, make your home in my heart. Amen.

Chapter 15

Carrying a Child—Bearing Christ

Inconveniences and burdens

> "If any want to become my followers, let them deny themselves and take up their cross and follow me."
>
> Matthew 16:24

There's nothing new or exotic about maternity. As long as there have been women, women have gone through pregnancy. All around the world and for thousands of years having babies has been the stuff of everyday human existence. Nonetheless, pregnancy continues to get our attention and hold it. Whether we are men or women, first-time mothers, experienced or adoptive mothers—or not even mothers at all—we find the process of pregnancy and birth strangely fascinating.

Childbirth is never old news. When it is happening to us or to someone we know, there is an aura of excitement in the air. Somehow, pregnancy always has the capacity to feel new all over again. I would have expected maternity to lose some of its flavor over time, but like a rarely used spice hidden in the back of a cupboard, I have found that with each pregnancy the taste has deepened and intensified. To my surprise—even after birthing seven children—maternity is every bit as awesome and full of wonder as it was the first time.

Trying to explain maternity to our older children has heightened my own sense of the mystery of it all. The truth is that when you begin to tell them how it all works, it sounds so outrageous and fantastical that you can hardly believe it yourself! I'll never forget the struck-by-lightning look on my pre-schooler's face when she finally grasped what I was telling her. Even third and fourth graders show glimmers of "I'm-not-sure-if-I-buy-this." The mix of joy and amazement they have expressed with the coming of each successive child has most definitely contributed to my own.

The wonders of pregnancy, however, do not negate its challenges. Maternity is never a breeze, even if and when it feels like one. I felt great when I was expecting our first child. I saw no reason whatsoever for treating pregnancy like an illness. And I couldn't understand why pregnant women were always being told to take care of themselves. That understanding came a few years later when I was a little older, a little wiser, and a bit less arrogant.

A model of self-sufficiency with that first pregnancy, I recall feeling exasperated by some of the well-intended but unsolicited advice people kept giving me. Even strangers seemed to come out of the woodwork touting their version of conventional wisdom, asking when I was due, and telling their own tales of family life. I have to admit that eventually I came to relish the extra attention and pampering that I received when I've been pregnant.

We receive extra consideration from family, friends, and even complete strangers because people recognize that pregnancy is, in a certain sense, burdensome. Those who notice that we are expecting respond to us in much the same way as they might when they see an elderly person board a crowded bus. Their kindness flows from the awareness that childbearing means *bearing* a child.

On a purely physical level, pregnancy requires us to put ourselves out. The child in the womb takes what he needs from our bodies, while we get only what's left over. Those gigantic vitamins we take are more for us than for our babies. They are prescribed because maternity depletes us.

While we make the day-to-day sacrifices of maternity without a second thought, we can easily fall out of touch with the very personal nature of those sacrifices. Many of us abstract what we are doing so much that we forget why we are doing it. No one in her right mind would volunteer to feel sick, gain weight, or carry around a bowling ball for several months. The reason we put ourselves out in these and so many more ways is not found in a principle or even in a process, but in a person. When our children grow up, we can look at each one of them and think, "I did that for you." By that time, however, we will have done so many more things that giving birth will seem almost small.

We put our own lives on the back burner not as an end in itself, but because that is what our children require. Pregnancy is a nine-month-long baby shower in which we give our babies our bodies and our lives. We count it a joy not because we are so holy or magnanimous, but because we love. That love is never general or indiscriminate. It is given by a particular woman to a particular child.

Sometimes I have found it difficult to remain conscious of the fact that no one is generically pregnant. I mean that none of us carries just *a* baby, or even *the* baby, but a completely unique and individual person within us. The changes we ourselves experience can distract us from thinking this way. We tend to lose our awareness of the fact that underneath all that belly is a *particular who* and not a *what.*

For Mary that *who* was the Son of God. The difficulties she faced were not exacted from her like some kind of payment to a divine creditor. The sacrifices she made were not part of some abstract spiritual exercise. What Mary bore—and it was plenty—was for love of *whom* Mary bore. She put her own desires and concerns on hold not because it was asked of her, but because *he* had asked it of her.

The Church proclaims Mary the *Theotokos* or God-bearer. Through her, God entered humanity. But Mary did not only bring Christ in to the world, she followed him as a disciple. Mary's total gift of herself to God is a mirror of God's sacrificial gift to us. Crucifixion was not his goal, *we* were. Because Jesus loved us, he bore our sins when he carried the cross. And long before Jesus carried the cross, Mary carried him.

We bear within our hearts not someone unknown to us, but that very same Christ. We are the objects of his love, a love which is no less personal than our own. This passionate love for us made his great sacrifice both meaningful and possible. Through it, Jesus not only carried a cross up a hill, but bore us and all we are up to heaven. He continues to give his life not only for us, but to us. It is that kind of loving sacrifice and self-denial that God invites us to embrace.

O Lord, our lives are filled with joy and wonder. Even in the most mundane and ordinary things, you are always giving us something new. You bury rich treasures in the rhythms of our days. You are forever showing us that there is so much more to life than what we can see.

Still Lord, I don't often bask in the wonder of your creation. My soul is drained with exhaustion. The bur-

dens that I carry weigh my spirit down. Sometimes I feel as if I cannot take one more step.

O Lord, when I grow tired, refresh me. When the sacrifices I make to follow you and the things I bear for the sake of others seem too much, help me. Set my heart aflame with the love that bears all things. Teach me to embrace the cross of your choosing and not to seek after what I would choose instead. As I carry your presence in my heart, help me to bear you to the world—even as you have borne me up to heaven. Amen.

Chapter 16

Centering on the Life Within

Getting and keeping perspective

Can a woman forget the nursing child,
or show no compassion for the child of her
  womb?
Even these may forget,
yet I will not forget you.
See, I have inscribed you on the palms of
  my hands...

Psalm 49:15–16

It's funny that when you have a new baby, it seems that you've had him or her forever. It doesn't take long for life without this child to be unimaginable. Pregnancy can have much the same quality. From the minute I first knew about each of our children, I could think of nothing else. Every waking moment—and many sleeping ones as well—were at least punctuated, if not dominated, by thoughts of the little stranger inside.

Regardless of what I was doing, "the baby" took center stage. Mentally, I'd maintain huge lists of all the things I needed to do. I'd interrupt myself to move furniture around in order to gain more space, and usually end by putting it back the way it was. Regular responsibilities took a back seat to sorting through clothes and toys with a vengeance. I shifted priorities and schedules to accommodate things that I had to get done B.B.—"Before Baby."

A strong sense of urgency often made me feel like there was something I had forgotten, or was about to forget. Never realizing just how preoccupied I was with the impending new arrival, I made all kinds of unconscious decisions. At the end of my first two pregnancies, I remember thinking that it would be unwise to start the laundry because labor might begin somewhere between the rinse cycle and the dryer. If I had actually continued with that line of logic, I would have ended up with a month's worth of dirty clothes to wash after I returned from the hospital. Thankfully, I did come to my senses before that happened.

During pregnancy not just our bodies, but our whole selves are busy tending to the new life within us. While our physical resources are focused on an unborn baby, our thoughts and feelings become fastened on his or her presence as well. We naturally begin to live our lives with reference to the someone else who is there, sometimes at the expense of other people and things that also deserve our attention.

Our babies, too, are captivated by us. Unlike the surrealistic photographs that occasionally grace the covers of magazines, an unborn child is not suspended in space. His or her whole world is his mother. Everything he or she can experience is mediated through her.

This kind of mutual absorption extends to the entire family. Older children make preparations of their own, and, while many won't admit it, fathers have plans too. Whether with joy or anxiety, new life quickly becomes the touchstone of our concerns.

In some ways the experience of preparing for a birth can be a lot like getting ready for Christmas. Baking, decorating, shopping, and wrapping packages—it seems like we will never get it all done. Though everything is done when the day comes, we can feel as if we have missed something. Perhaps it is because we have.

Sadly, I have to admit that in my earlier pregnancies a great deal of my preparations remained primarily material. I bought diapers and clothes; we set up a crib and made decisions about feeding and our use of time and money. We *did* all the *things* that needed to be done.

With later pregnancies, I came to the conclusion that crossing all those indispensable necessities off the list accomplishes very little in terms of genuine preparation. Somehow, all that stuff gets done anyway; and it's no sin to set up a crib while mother and baby are still in the hospital. No doubt the diapers are important, but even more important is creating the spiritual and emotional readiness to welcome a new baby home. These are deeper preparations.

The Scriptures tell us precious little about the plans Mary made for the birth of her Son. Certainly, there were fewer options to entertain and fewer choices to be made. Mary didn't have to decided between bottle or breast, cloth or disposable, "natural" or with anesthesia. However, what has always surprised me is that it seems no one had made arrangements in Bethlehem for the birth itself!

It could appear that Mary was not a very well-organized young mother. Nevertheless, I think that she was more prepared for the birth of her child than most of us have ever been for ours. When Mary says, "Behold, I am the handmaid of the Lord" (Lk 1:38), it is clear that she has prepared her heart.

Mary was ready to receive whatever God would give because her life was centered on him. The Lord had been the focus of her thoughts and emotions and choices all along. Now, her physical and material existence would be centered on God's Son. Mary was prepared to accept anything. We hear it in her voice when she says, "May it be with me according to your word" (Lk 1:38).

While we can only guess at Mary's preparations, the accounts of God's preparations for the birth of Christ are innumerable. Through prophets and kings, by law and by sacrifice, in slavery, exile, and persecution, God had carefully planned his coming. The entire history of humankind records God's work to make not only a virgin, but a people and a world ready to receive his Son.

God did not prepare only the birth of Jesus in Bethlehem. Perhaps there was no room in Bethlehem's inn because that was not the room God had been preparing. Jesus did not come to be born in an inn or stable, but in our hearts. The Father did not shower his attentions on Jesus, but on us. God's love, though centered *in* Christ, centers *on* us.

It's almost comic to think of a pregnant woman forgetting the baby she carries. (No one who sees her does!) We all know that even when we try, it's nearly impossible to ignore the presence of another person once we know they are present. And yet, it is so easy to forget God, who dwells in our hearts. I, for one, seem to have no trouble at all being distracted from God, even when I'm making a real effort to tune him in.

We sense one another's presence every day. Intimacy, however, depends on what we do with what we sense. That is true whether we are talking about intimacy with an unborn child, one another, or with God. We all set the boundaries of our relationships. We can limit the intimacy of our encounters if we choose to do so. When we do, we live our lives more *alongside* others than genuinely *with* them.

Knowing that God is centered on us, Mary centered herself on God. Our faith empowers us to do the same.

We are so easily absorbed by the presence of a child in the womb. But we can learn to be similarly captivated by the divine presence that stirs in our hearts. It happens when we choose and foster an inner awareness.

There are too many distractions to the life of faith. More often than not, we need to take shelter from the whirlwind of exterior life that surrounds us. When we do, we can draw from the interior life of the Spirit that is at the core of our being. We can do this even while we are attending to all the things we must do. The secret lies in choosing the better part: that is, in deliberately centering ourselves on the One who already lives at the center of our deepest selves.

O God, you are ever present beneath this thin crust that forms the surface of my life. On my right and on my left, above and below, before and behind, you surround me with your love. Within my very heart, you dwell with me always. Lord, I give so much of my attention to what is shallow, immediate, and passing. Sometimes I ignore you and go about my business as if you weren't even there. Sometimes when I seek you, I look everywhere but in my own soul.

Lord, teach me to live my life with reference to you alone and with reverence for your life in others. Teach me how to enter within my own soul, and help me to find you at the very center of my heart. Steal me away from all distractions, and captivate me with your loving presence. Prepare my life to receive you, and help me to choose you over all else. Amen.

Chapter 17

Worry

Misplaced trust

"Do not let your hearts be troubled. Believe in God, believe also in me."
John 14:1

I remember waking up late one morning shortly after bringing our first baby home. Looking at the clock, I thought something had to be wrong. I hadn't been disturbed all night, and the baby should have been up three hours before! What in the world happened?

Fearing the worst, I ran to the crib to see if she was still alive and breathing. I was hardly able to breathe myself. My heart was thumping. I felt like I had been caught up in a whirlwind. When I got to the crib, I found the baby blissfully asleep.

A small departure from routine had tripped my interior alarm. Her sleeping through the night was all it took to trigger an emotional response that quickly had a life of its own. You'd think that I would have learned from that experience, but I have to admit repeating that same scene with at least three or four of our other children.

Sometimes there is real cause for concern. When I was five months along with our oldest son, a speeding drunk driver hit our car while we were stopped at a light. The impact was so great that hats and shoes flew off. The glass from the rear window was shattered all over the street. Our two girls seemed all right, but we were very shaken. All I could think about was losing my baby, having miscarried less than a year before.

When the ambulance arrived, we were put on boards and rushed to the hospital. For the sake of the girls, I knew I had to act calmly even if I wasn't really calm. In truth, I was pretty much a basket case. The hospital staff hooked me up to a fetal monitor, and hearing that little heart beating regularly flooded me with tears of relief. Except for some sore necks and backs, all of us were fine. I realized that I had learned how to worry.

Worry was something quite new to me, having been a rather carefree child growing up. In fact, it had always bothered me to see how much anxiety my mother had. I often vowed to myself (loud enough for my mother to hear), that I would never become a "worry wart." That was a promise easy to keep—until I became a mother myself. Now that some of our children have reached their teens, I've stopped pretending otherwise.

Worry seems to be part of a mother's job description. Whether the circumstances prompting our anxiety are justified or not, the underlying reason is the same. In wanting the best for our children, we find plenty of things to be anxious about. We especially worry about situations we cannot control. We can worry so much that we end up being out of control ourselves.

Most of us live our daily lives acting as if everything is in our hands. Even if we know how short our reach is, we're still shocked when something happens to us that is beyond our influence. The fact is that a lot of us deeply desire to run our own lives, and anything that flies in the face of that desire causes us great consternation.

It's tempting to think that Mary had no real concerns. After all, her child was the Son of God. Surely, God would take care of everything. From the outside it can look very much like Mary "had it made," that she didn't worry because she had nothing to worry about.

In truth, Mary had at least as much to worry about as her contemporaries. To begin with, she lived at a time and in a culture that did not welcome unwed mothers with open arms, but with stones in hand. Being pregnant under those circumstances was a definite cause for anxiety. Mary had a lot of explaining to do, especially to Joseph. They both knew the child wasn't his. Betrothal would offer her protection, but not if Joseph rejected her. Perhaps Joseph didn't have the heart to have her stoned, but he may not have had the will to take her into his house either. Had that been the case—without a man to provide for her— Mary would have been destitute. Even widows, if they had no sons, were left with no financial standing whatsoever. A woman's social position was entirely dependent on the status of the man who cared for her. Mary did not have the option of being self-supporting. No one would have done business with her.

Mary had absolutely no control over the circumstances of her life, but she did not let fear or anxiety cripple her. Mary may have felt some worry when difficult circumstances swirled around her, but she did not allow herself to be overcome. Rather, she discerned that she could rest secure in the hand of God. She trusted that God was in control, and believed that her Lord would not let her down.

We all know that worry accomplishes nothing. Nevertheless, we spend a great deal of ourselves in nervous desperation. Perhaps when we worry, it's not because we don't trust anything, but because we have trusted the *wrong* thing. There are instances in all our lives when we relied too heavily on a check in the mail, a medical exam, a family member, or even ourselves. Anxiety erupts when we stubbornly place our trust in anything other than God.

Worry can poison our lives. It steals our joy and our freedom; it fosters discontent—it can even make us physically ill. Moreover, it undermines our faith by convincing us that God isn't powerful or attentive enough to take care of our needs, maybe even that God isn't faithful.

The voice of worry tells us to take over the wheel, but, instead, we are invited to sit back and enjoy the ride. God begs us to look at the lilies of the field and the birds of the air. They do not toil or spin, nor do they sow or reap, and yet he cares for them (cf. Mt 6:26, 28). God asks us to consider for a moment what it would be like if we really *did* control our own lives and destinies. Maybe, just maybe, it would be more frightening than simply allowing God to do so!

When we find ourselves worried, we can't just wait it out; we have to take it someplace. And the place for anxiety is prayer. The Scriptures teach us that while we shouldn't "worry about anything" (Phil 4:6), we should also "pray without ceasing" (1 Thes 5:17). God promises us peace not when we struggle to hold on to whatever concerns us, but when we allow our loving Lord to hold us in his loving arms.

God encourages us not to worry, but to pray for our children. The Lord assures us that when we are not in control he is. Our God tells us that all we need do is ask, seek, and knock—to come to the Father in confidence with every concern. There is nothing that lies beyond the power of prayer or beyond the power of God's love. Instead of misplacing our trust in ourselves, how much wiser it is to place our trust in the One who loves us best!

O Lord, how self-sufficient and independent I think I am! How foolishly I pretend that I can plan every step I take and author every chapter of my life! How readily I mount life like a horse, believing that I hold the reins!

When I find myself unequal to the task, the facade falls around me. I see that I can no longer trust in myself, and yet I find it difficult to trust in you. The storms that rage around me sometimes rage within me. I can be overcome by anxiety and fear. The reality of my powerlessness frightens me.

Teach me, O God, to know my weakness, so that I may learn to know your strength. Show me that there is nothing beyond your reach. Pull every false support out from under me until I place my life completely in your hands. Keep me at rest in the power of your faithful love. Teach me to be anxious for nothing and to pray always. Amen.

Chapter 18

The Unspeakable "What-Ifs"

Addressing our fears

> "For he makes his sun rise on the evil and on the good, and sends rain on the righteous and on the unrighteous."
>
> Matthew 6:7

Although I don't remember ever discussing aloud my concerns for the health of my children, I do recall a series of nightmares I had during my first few pregnancies. In these dreams, the baby would be born prematurely and then diagnosed with some terrible illness or condition. One night it would be Down's syndrome, another spina bifida, or cerebral palsy. Over the course of a few weeks, I went through almost every illness I could name.

The dreams were so vivid, I began to wonder if they were premonitions. To make it worse, almost every conversation I had about my new baby seemed to end with the same refrain: boy or girl, cute or ugly, gifted or just one of the crowd, nothing really mattered "as long as it's healthy!"

But what if my baby wasn't healthy? What if there was something wrong—even something seriously wrong? I began to ask myself just what I'd do and how I'd feel if my baby wasn't "normal." I wasn't sure that I liked my answers much at all.

Most of us wonder if our children will be healthy and if not what we will do. We all hope for the best, but at the same time we know that for some mothers these hopes will be disappointed. For the most part, our fears remain unvoiced.

It isn't pleasant to think about the lives of families with children who are not well. While we admire their courage, most of us keep our distance. We do everything we can to hold onto the belief that it can't happen to us. We tell ourselves that the deck is stacked in our favor. After all, those things only happen to people who can handle them—and we can't.

Suffering makes us uncomfortable. It seems beyond our grasp to understand or even explain. In particular, a child who suffers presents us with a most acute dilemma. We shake our fists at heaven when we see a child in pain.

It is hard for me to admit how much I take for granted and how ungrateful I can be. In some ways, I suppose we all think we deserve nothing less than a "perfect" child. The problem lies in what we mean by "perfect." In the beginning we may think that a perfect baby is one who has ten fingers and ten toes. Later, a whole host of requirements begin entering into our assessments of our children. In some sense every child and no child is "perfect." Human limitations and deficits appear in every one of us, but so do wonderfully inspiring qualities and gifts. As important as good health is, it is not a ticket to a life without difficulties. The inverse, however, is also true. Life can be lived with dignity and joy, even in the midst of difficult health issues.

Most of us would agree—if we thought about it—that we deserve suffering no more than we deserve blessing. But underneath the rational thoughts, we might hear an inner voice telling us that if there is something wrong, we are somehow to blame. Sometimes we mistakenly connect suffering with sin, thinking of it as some kind of divine pay-back—a deserved sentence for a committed offense. Like those followers of Jesus who encountered the man born blind, we can find ourselves asking, "Who sinned, this man or his parents?" (Jn 9:2).

If we insist on this point of view, however, we would be rather unfair to God, who is so rich in mercy. The Lord does not send suffering upon his children. While he may well bring good from it, suffering is not part of God's plan. Nonetheless, we may wonder why an all-powerful God would stand by and allow a child—life's greatest joy—to become life's greatest trial.

Most of us respond to suffering in our lives with a shout of "Why me?" Perhaps the deepest answer to that question is the one that is the simplest: "Why not?" No one of us is exempt from pain. No matter how good someone may seem to have it—and no matter how good someone may seem to be—everyone has a load to bear. A cross always looks lighter when someone else is carrying it.

Suffering tempts us to give it more power over us that it actually has. We give it more power if we let it distort and dominate our perspective. A child with an illness has a set of difficulties others may not have. Whatever the diagnosis, however, we don't give birth to problems, but to children. The problems may be terrible, but the child is always good. That is why, when I was over thirty-five and still having children, I chose not to undergo standard prenatal diagnostic testing. If my baby was going to have serious health concerns, I wanted to see the child first—and not the diagnosis. I believed that if I could accept the child, then I could accept any illness that might follow. If I could lovingly embrace the child as my own, then I could find the strength to do whatever I would need to do in that loving embrace. Love would strengthen love.

Of course others have benefited greatly from knowing if a child is facing difficult health issues. More and more can be done medically even before birth to reduce or even eliminate severe or threatening conditions. Families may be better prepared to attend to a child's individual needs if they know about them in advance.

Whether we know about health issues in advance or not, the particular challenges we may face with a child who is ill do not have to interfere with the love we share. At root, the human capacity to love and be loved remains constant. The quality of a person's life is determined more by the quality of the *person* than by the quality of the *life*.

While suffering disturbs us at the deepest levels, it is important that while we struggle with it we find a way toward peace and acceptance. Perhaps in small, even imperceptible steps, faith can slowly grow in the places once occupied by fears. Our faith teaches us that in our trials there is not only the hidden presence of God, but also a hidden opportunity for growth in the pain. We want and need to believe that suffering can somehow make sense; Christian discipleship assures us that it can. Suffering can be redemptive.

As difficult as it is to accept our hardships and those of our children, we must remember that God's only Son wasn't spared either. If anyone in history didn't deserve to suffer it was Jesus. Nonetheless, his whole mission—the redemption of the world—was accomplished through his suffering. It was not senseless, but full of both life and meaning for us.

Both God and Mary owned a portion of that suffering too. Mary felt the sword pierce her heart as would any mother. Yet, she was able to stand at the foot of the cross because God's grace flowed from it. Ultimately, she experienced the fruit of that tree as life not as death. God, on the other hand, found his greatest solidarity with us in the sufferings of Jesus. Through the passion and death of Christ, God shared fully in the human condition. In Christ's resurrection, we are now able to share his glory.

The cross of Christ makes clear to us that suffering never comes alone. When it comes, it is always accompanied by the grace to bear it, as well as a gift to rejoice in. Strange as it may seem, we call the awful day of crucifixion "Good Friday." We do so because we have found wrapped in the greatest suffering imaginable a gift beyond imagination. That gift can dispel even our deepest fears.

Healthy or not, every child remains a gift. Most of us have heard the parents of children with poor medical prognoses express how those children have enriched their lives. They teach us to delight in life itself, and to recognize it all as miraculous. In bearing heavy burdens with surprising joy, these parents show us that it is possible to look beyond an illness and see both a child and the One who gives all children.

The cross is not a place where any of us wants to be. But at the cross, we may begin to understand the answer Jesus gave regarding suffering. To those who asked about the man born blind, Jesus said, "Neither this man nor his parents sinned; he was born blind so that God's works might be revealed in him" (Jn 9:3).

Lord, there are so many things I take for granted and so many blessings I have left uncounted. I have gone about so much of my life hoping for fairy-tale endings and happily-ever-afters. Sometimes I've even convinced myself that I deserve nothing less.

Yet, underneath it all, I know how frail life can be, and how even small matters can cast long shadows. I am afraid of what suffering may challenge me to bear, and so I run away from what it offers me. I am all too ready to take the blame, but far too hesitant to accept the cross.

Lord, help me not to turn away from my own pain or the pain of others. Teach me to see the redemption that you offer there. Reveal to me, O God, your hidden glory; and give me the grace to look beyond the suffering into your compassionate face. Amen.

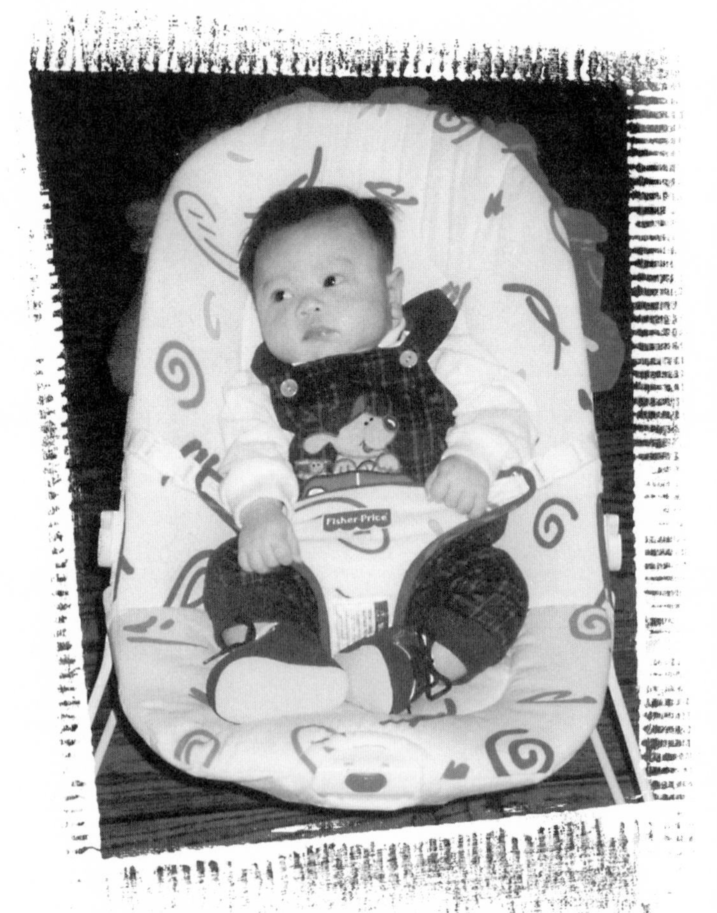
Fisher Price

Chapter 19

Broken Promises

Miscarriage

"The Lord gave, and the Lord has taken away; blessed be the name of the Lord."
Job 1:21

If having a child is one of our greatest joys, losing a child is as great a sorrow. Although we don't like to think about it, not every pregnancy ends with birth. A great number of women experience a miscarriage sometime during their reproductive years. I have met elderly women, even those who have raised several children, who have told me they still think about the babies they lost.

I remember the date of my miscarriage as readily as I do the birth dates of my children. It happened two months into my third pregnancy. I went to the airport to pick up a friend who was visiting for the weekend.

When I stopped at the bathroom, I discovered that I was bleeding.

Shaking and crying, I ran to a telephone to call my husband at work. I immediately left for home. He called the doctor and picked up our friend at the airport. I knew every pregnancy was different, but nothing like this had ever happened to me before.

I stayed in bed, hoping the bleeding would stop or at least slow down. My doctor met us at the hospital the next morning. He told me that I would have to wait it out, but that I hadn't lost the baby yet. He also told me that if I did miscarry, I would know it. The chances were about fifty-fifty.

I did everything I could think of to save my baby. I stayed in bed. I spent a lot of time on the phone consulting a friend who had been through a miscarriage the previous month. I tried to stay positive and muster all the hope I could. I did a lot of praying.

My physical condition did improve a little, but my emotional state continued to deteriorate. I felt as if I was in a suspended state of emergency. The siren had sounded, the bell had rung, but there was nothing I could do to stop whatever was happening.

While the alarm continued to ring in my ears, everyone around me seemed calm. For them, time would tell. But for me, the turmoil and the waiting was more than I could stand.

My doctor scheduled an ultrasound a few days later. I had never had one with my other two pregnancies, so I wasn't sure what to expect. He told me that what we were hoping to find was "a smudge with a beat."

During the procedure, the technician seemed puzzled. When my doctor called later that day, I found out why. The sonogram showed absolutely no sign of pregnancy. My womb was empty and clean. There wasn't any need for a D&C. I had, in fact, miscarried. The baby was gone without a trace, and so was the hope I had held on to.

The pain of that loss did not draw our family together. Rather, each of us sought his or her own means of coping with it. I knew that my husband and children were deeply disappointed. Nevertheless, they all seemed able to accept it. Knowing that I had miscarried was not the resolution they wanted; but for them it *was* a resolution. The pregnancy was over, and the miscarriage was over too.

For me, however, the grief had just begun. There were no mixed emotions or confused feelings for me to sort out. There was just sadness, deep sadness like an aching emptiness nothing could relieve. I knew that my baby hadn't just disappeared. He had died. And worse, it had happened inside me.

I kept thinking that everything would be better "tomorrow," but "tomorrow" never came. Everyone expected me to get over it. But every time I saw a pregnant woman the wound opened up all over again. I'm sure I never saw so many pregnant women in all my life. It seemed like they had all come out of the woodwork just to spite me. I was angry, too, at myself, and at God for allowing the miscarriage to happen. Now it seemed as though God was adding insult to injury. Whatever I did, I could not get out from under the lonely dark cloud that hung over me.

Despite the well-intentioned people who tried to comfort me, I felt completely alone. Some encouraged me to be grateful for the two children I already had. Many told me that the miscarriage was a "blessing in disguise," that there had probably been something very wrong with my baby anyway. They reminded me that I was young and sure to get pregnant again. Nothing people said to me helped. For the most part, I think it made things worse.

I couldn't get past the feeling that no one around me "got it." It seemed that people were unwilling to treat my miscarriage as what it actually was—the loss of a child. Of course I was grateful for the daughters I already had. If anything, the miscarriage had made me more grateful, not less. I knew that my baby may have had serious problems that had contributed to or even caused the miscarriage. The pain, however, wasn't any less real. He was mine, and I already loved him. I also knew that I might well have other children in the future, but that is what they would be: *other* children. This child, this individual, was lost to me forever.

I don't know what it's like to lose a child who has already lived as part of a family. I cannot even come close to imagining the enormity of that kind of pain.

Most of us have not even seen the unborn children we have lost, let alone held them, cared for them, or enjoyed them as individuals. Many seem to think that this relative detachment lessens the loss. But in my own experience of miscarriage, it was precisely these unfulfilled expectations—these broken promises—that hurt most.

Days passed, but I couldn't stop crying. I didn't weep for the loss of a relationship I had, but for one I would never have. The grief I experienced was rooted in what might have been—what should have been—and not in what was. I regretted that my baby and I would never have the chance to become what we were meant to be to each other.

Having nowhere else to turn, I began to pray. Instead of praying for my baby, I began to ask him to pray with me. I was convinced that I had been carrying a boy, so I named him Paul, after the friend I had gone to meet at the airport. I poured out my grief to him and to God over what had happened. I told him that I loved him, that I had wanted him very much, and that I missed him terribly. I trusted that he was now with God. Gradually, the darkness began to lift.

Although it was true that my baby was gone, I realized that I had let the miscarriage rob me of more than my child. My pain had eclipsed the relationship I had with my lost child. I had allowed myself to experience the reality of the loss, but had distanced myself from the reality of the child.

The intensity of the loss had made everything seem like such a waste. But when I pursued my child spiritually, the value of his life became clear. Naming my baby and praying with him preserved the relationship that death could not steal. Suddenly, Paul's life became more to me than just the few weeks he had lived inside me. He was more than a miscarriage, a mistake, or a footnote. He was a child of mine alive in the presence of the God who had created him.

However short his life, I began to understand that Paul was God's gift to me just as my other children were. The quality of the gift was not diminished by the fact that we had so little time together. We belong to one another for all eternity. Paul is a member of our family. Our joy in heaven will be greater because of our loss on earth.

It has been many years since my miscarriage, but I still think about Paul—not every day, but often. I wonder how our family would have been different if he had been born. The grief is mostly gone. But Paul's gift remains undimmed. Losing Paul taught me that even when it doesn't seem like it, God is faithful. Our Lord does not break his promises. Even in the midst of the pain and disappointment of what looked like an unfulfilled promise of new life, God was there. God is with us and for us. God is never lost to us. Sickness and death may snatch us away from one another, but nothing can snatch us out of the Lord's hand. In the end, we will find each other there—where we will see what God is forever trying to show us. Even in loss, there is gain.

O Lord, you are gracious to me beyond measure. You shower me with good gifts. You fill my cup to overflowing. You withhold nothing from me. I have most everything that I need.

Lord, you are a God with two hands: one that gives and one that takes away. You freely give so that I might learn to freely receive; and sometimes you take, so that I might learn to give.

Father, do not let the pain of loss isolate me from others or from you. Teach me instead to reach out to others and to draw ever closer to your heart. Help me to hold you even more dear than what you have given me—dearer too than all I may have lost. Show me that what I lose is only for a time, but that what I gain in you is eternal. For all things are passing, Lord, except you; and in you, I possess all things. Amen.

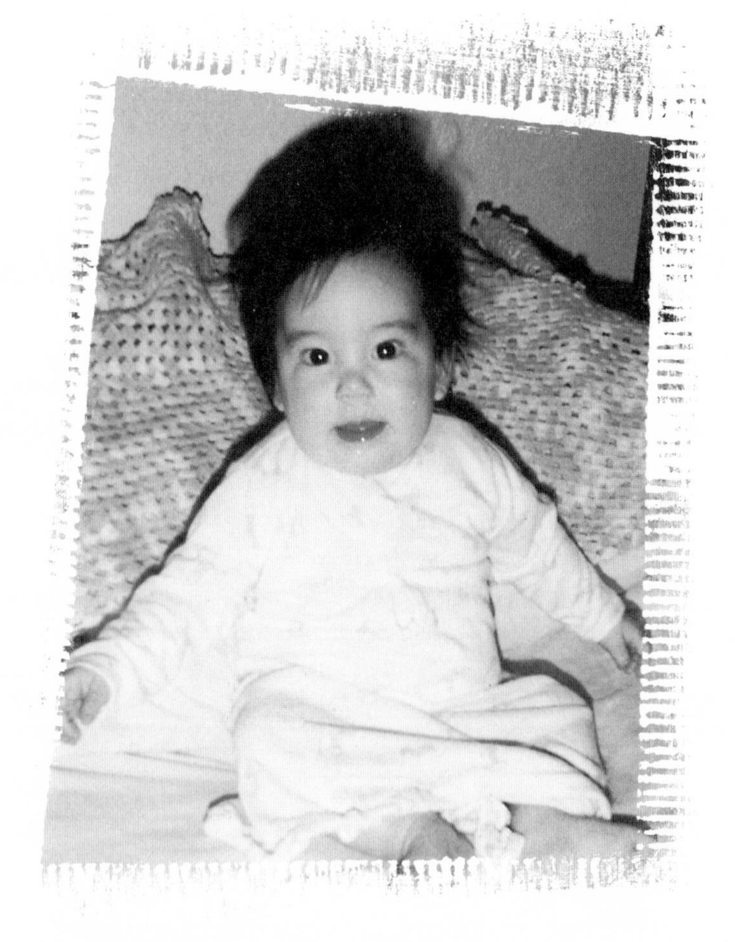

Chapter 20

Growing Together

Expanding our hearts

> O Lord my God, you are very great.
> You stretch out the heavens like a tent.
> Psalm 103:1, 2

At my very first visit to the obstetrician, I was told that my bone structure made me a very good candidate for a cesarean section. According to my doctor, any baby much over seven pounds could prove beyond my ability to deliver "naturally." Believing that God and nature did a pretty good job taking care of these things, I wasn't particularly upset. The fact that I had weighed under six pounds at birth myself gave me reason to expect a small baby. I figured that I had little cause for concern.

What I didn't realize, though, was just how big any baby really is. When they are newborns, even the big ones look small. But before they are born, even the small babies are quite sizable. To my surprise, it wasn't too long before I filled what had seemed like unnecessary room in my maternity clothes. Both my baby and I grew at breakneck speed. The baby stretched to fill all the available space, and I stretched to make more space available.

And it wasn't just my belly that got bigger. Everything grew: arms and ankles, face and feet. In fact, having always had a rather girlish figure, it was quite shocking for me to go up three bra sizes in just six weeks!

All that stretching did not come without pain or discomfort. Muscles I didn't know I had ached under the stress. Discovering heartburn, water retention, and stretch marks—I couldn't help but wonder just how much anyone could stretch before bursting at the seams! Nonetheless, when all was said and done, I delivered our first daughter at nine pounds, eleven ounces—without a C-section. Eventually, I even managed to deliver our largest newborn, at eleven pounds, eight ounces! He didn't even fit in the hospital's nursery clothes.

My body, however, wasn't the only thing that needed to be stretched. Obviously, my babies depended on my physical ability to stretch to accommodate them as they grew. But far beyond the nine months before birth, they would depend on me to stretch my heart for them as well. I would have to learn to nurture them not just with my body, but with my whole life.

Maternity stretches a woman inside and out. While our bodies grow openly and publicly, our hearts do so in secret. The inner stretches of the soul are neither less astonishing nor less painful than the outward and more visible ones. But unlike the swelling of the womb with child, most of the inner growth we experience is not temporary or passing. We are forever altered by it. We are never again the same as before. After eight pregnancies, I know that single-digit dress sizes are probably gone for me forever. It is my hope, however, that single-digit soul sizes are gone as well.

Love requires us to stretch for one another. The call to expand our hearts is not for mothers only. It resounds in every family as a whole. With each new addition, parents must learn to divide their energies, and older children must learn to share and to wait. Most families with more than one child know how difficult these lessons can be. But it seems that children have a special elasticity of spirit. I have seen few things more beautiful than an older sister kissing her younger brother's bruised knee, or a baby at home running to the door to greet older children as they return from school. Families are, indeed, where we learn to love.

As the days and weeks of Mary's pregnancy passed, she blossomed just like the rest of us. Her young body, filled with new life, had to stretch to accommodate her child. But Mary's heart, and her life, had to expand even more. Her pregnancy, after all, was unique. So, too, was her child. For this obscure and provincial teenager, life would change dramatically. This child would bring her both attention and adversity. Because of him, Mary would travel to Bethlehem, escape to Egypt, settle in Galilee, and ultimately stand beneath a cross. Through it all, Mary stretched and grew. As the Scriptures tell us, she "treasured all these things in her heart" (Lk 2:51).

At first glance, the significance of that one day of the annunciation seems to take on enormous proportions. It is tempting to identify the angel's visit as the obvious turning point which would define and direct Mary's life. But to do so would be to ignore the secret inner life of Mary's soul that brought her there. What changed Mary's life was not a single moment or event, but the unparalleled intimacy she shared with God. It is the reflection of that intimacy which gives luster to the moment of the annunciation.

Mary's relationship with God did not begin with the angel's message, nor was it co-conceived with Jesus. It was because she had mothered and nurtured the Holy Spirit in her heart, that Mary fulfilled God's purpose for her life. The divine presence grew in her soul long before and long after the Son grew as a child in her womb.

It is not Mary's, but our intimacy with God that has its beginnings at the annunciation. Through her willingness to open her life to the Son of God, Mary brought Jesus to us. Further, her life of grace shows us what it means to be stretched and formed by the indwelling presence of the Divine Stranger. Because

Mary centered her life on nurturing God's life within her, God was not a stranger.

People, and not things, both cause and enable our personal growth. They are often the source of our greatest challenges as well as our deepest joys. But we do not accord everyone in our lives equal influence. We don't stretch for a stranger as we do for a friend, nor for a friend as we do for a family member. The degree of intimacy determines the degree to which someone will be able to shape and foster our growth. Our bodies stretch for our unborn children because they are inside us. Our hearts and lives stretch for them because our children reach to the core of our inner beings.

Although bearing the child Jesus was a privilege reserved for Mary alone, like Mary, we all bear God's presence in the womb of our hearts. We know that a child in the womb cannot sustain growth and development without our nurturing and mothering. Most of us do everything we can to ensure that our unborn children are being nurtured properly. But somehow many of us lose sight of the need to nurture Christ in our hearts. Focusing exclusively on our identity as children of God, we sometimes do not see our need to mother the divine life that God plants within us. We need to feed the life of Christ with our own lives, just as we feed our unborn children with our bodies.

The life of faith is a life of growth. As our children grow to fill more and more of our bodies and lives, so Christ longs to fill our hearts. If we think that we are too small to bear the God who cannot be contained by heaven and earth, we are right. But the intimacy God seeks stretches and expands us. As we mother God's growth in us, the Holy One will swell our hearts until they are big enough to embrace him fully.

Lord, how great you are indeed! How deep, and how high, and how vast you are! There is no created thing big enough to hold you, for in just one hand you hold all things. Yet your greatness, Lord, seeks out the small. Your love for the poor and the weak draws you to me.

But Lord, I am too small to be your home. Whatever space I have inside me is crammed full of myself. My soul is crowded by worldly concerns. My mind is frenzied with distractions of every kind. and my life is cluttered at times with vain and useless pursuits.

Stretch me, O God, and swell my heart. Make me a tent of your dwelling. Empty my soul of all that keeps me from others and from you. Teach me to nurture the seed you have planted, and to feed your life within me with your own. Shape me, O Lord, and mold me from within. Grow in my heart and fill me until I can contain you no more. Amen.

Chapter 21

Eating—and Everything Else—for Two

Self-sacrifice and self-gift

Present your bodies as a living sacrifice, holy and acceptable to God, which is your spiritual worship.

Romans 12:1

One summer afternoon shortly before we knew we were expecting our oldest son, I came home from my weekly trip to the grocery store. As I set about unpacking the bags, our two girls began to giggle and laugh. I couldn't imagine what could be so funny until I saw that the kitchen table was piled with lime gelatin, lime sherbet, limeade mix, and fresh limes. I hadn't intended to buy all those lime related things. Nonetheless, there they were! There was something strangely familiar about that kind of irrational behavior, but I couldn't put my finger on what it was. A few weeks

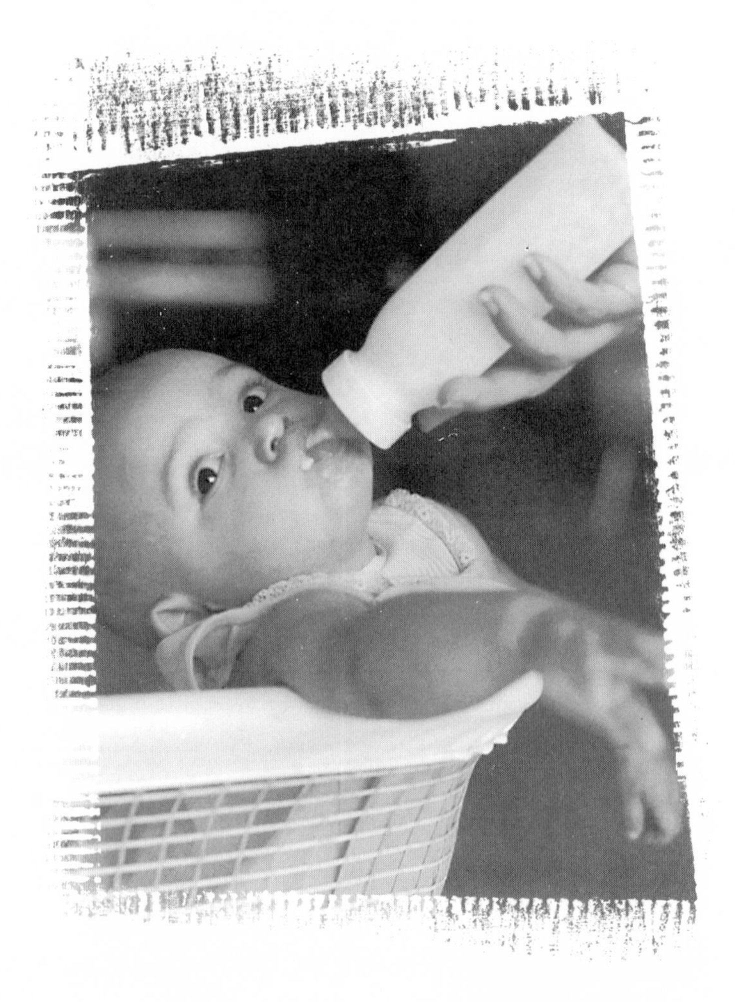

later, however, the pieces fell into place and we all knew why I had been feeling a little green!

Most of us have stories to tell about what we eat during pregnancy. The cravings we commonly experience seem to come out of the blue, but when they hit, they are a force to be reckoned with. I remember waking up one morning with Stove Top stuffing on my mind. Hoping it would pass, I tried to go about my daily routine. Nevertheless, no matter what I did, I just couldn't stop thinking about stuffing. I tried to stave it off by eating lots of carrot sticks. I crusaded against excessive self-indulgence, but to no avail. By suppertime it had become so intense that I finally broke down and consumed a virtual mountain of stuffing.

Our dietary exploits during pregnancy often involve how much we eat as well as what we eat. One would think that a woman with child would have less room in her stomach for food, but I, for one, have never been able to pack it in like I can when I am pregnant. Many of us absolutely dread stepping on that merciless scale month after month. I still dread it, even if no one is looking. I always tried to soften the blow by deducting a generous allowance for my clothing—you know, five or ten pounds! Despite my sometimes valiant efforts to limit what and how much I ate, I held the record at my doctor's office for weight gain in a single month at fourteen pounds. (Not even my biggest baby weighed *that* much!)

Humorous as they may be, maternal cravings serve a purpose. They are concrete expressions of our children's needs. I didn't need the limes or carrots—and certainly not six servings of stuffing—but somehow, the baby inside me did. Mysteriously and without words, he communicated his needs to me, and filled them through me. And regardless of my older children's giggles, my husband's raised eyebrows, or my doctor's infernal scale, I could easily justify exotic foods and enormous portions. After all, I was "eating for two."

The fact is that when we're pregnant we do much more than just eat for two. We breathe, rest, and we hope, pray for two as well. Indeed, we actually live for two. Our children cannot care for themselves, so we do for them most of what they need. But if we are to meet our children's physical, emotional, and spiritual needs, we must also give them our lives and sacrifice our wants for the sake of their needs.

Although all sacrifice is a kind of death, we are not like the sacrificial animals once offered on temple altars. We do not die for our children, we live for them. We cannot fulfill our love for them with a single act of offering, but perpetually with the thousands of small self-denials that fill a lifetime. We make our whole lives a gift to our children. In so doing, we become living sacrifices for them.

Many of us like to think of ourselves as independent and self-reliant, but in truth we are not much different from our unborn children. In struggling to provide for our children, we invariably discover that we are unable to provide for all of our own needs. Even those who are the most successful at supplying material necessities may be at a loss when it comes to satisfying the emotional or spiritual hungers we share.

Common to each of us is a hunger for something more, something else, something deeper. We may not know what—or rather whom—we need. We may not even realize that we need anything or anyone at all. But in some way, all of us exhibit an inner restlessness of spirit. Those who deny the hunger of the heart starve their souls. Others perceive it, but may not know just how to address it. Whether we choose to ignore or address our spiritual needs, however, they do not go unexpressed in our lives.

Frequently the inner cravings of the soul are articulated in the spiritual equivalents of pickles and ice cream. If we do not understand the nature of our inner needs, we may try to fill them by sampling the full range of exotic "spiritual" experiences. On the other hand, we may attempt to substitute what we cannot supply with vast quantities of material things we *are* able to acquire for ourselves. Ultimately, though, we all find that we cannot be satisfied by our own poor efforts. Just as when we crave one food and try to satisfy ourselves with another, we are left hungry.

It is in Christ alone, and through him, that all our needs can be expressed and filled. Just as the child in the womb must rely on his mother to give voice to his needs, we depend on Jesus to intercede for us. He does so in the Spirit, "with inexpressible groanings" (cf. Rom 8:26). He knows that we are too weak to care for our souls adequately. Jesus understands that we cannot supply ourselves with what we need, because our deepest need is for him.

Our lives are not only our own. Family life teaches us that we belong to one another, and that we depend on one another. Similarly, our hearts are not just ours. Our spirits are restless precisely because we are made not only by God, but also for God. We cry out from the bottomless pit of our human hearts because only God can satisfy our hearts.

We can do nothing to acquire God for ourselves. Yet, our Lord is always ready to give himself to us. We give our children what they need from our bodies and our lives. Likewise, God gives everything to those who ask—and a great deal to those who don't bother to ask! Jesus tells us that our heavenly Father knows what we need even before we ask. He teaches us not to worry for food or clothing or shelter. Again and again God promises to "fully satisfy every need of yours according to his riches in glory in Christ Jesus" (Phil 4:19).

Nevertheless, the life of faith is not a one-way street, where we ask and receive, and God listens and gives. For although without need, God is not without desires. God hungers for intimacy. The very existence of creation expresses this divine longing. In the beginning, the Creator made all things for himself. The Father created men and women in the divine image to be his friends. Our Lord desired us even when we rejected his love. From the moment of our fall from grace, God prepared our salvation to restore the intimacy we had discarded.

Human need and divine desire meet in the person and work of Jesus Christ. In him, God became a living and eternal sacrifice for us. God became one *of* us, in order to become one *with* us. It is God's desire for intimacy, and not ours, that leads and directs us deeper in faith. Like a child in the womb who motivates us to do what we must to fill her needs, it is Christ, alive in our hearts, who draws us closer to him. There is nothing that can take our place with the Lord. No tree or ocean or mountain can satisfy God's craving for intimacy with every man and woman. Only our hearts can fill the hunger of Christ.

Lord, it is good that you know all our needs even before we ask, for if I came to you with all of them, my prayer would never end! I am completely dependent on your loving kindness. My home, my food, my family, my work—all of these are from you.

Yet, Lord, my restless heart betrays a deeper need. My soul thirsts within me. My flesh craves for something more that I cannot grasp for myself.

Give me yourself, Lord, for I cannot take you. Give me yourself, O God, or my soul will starve. More than food and shelter, Lord, I need you to fill and protect me. Strengthen my faith, and give me eyes to see the needs of others. Teach me to embrace you not only in need, but in love. Let me desire you as you desire me that I might fill your hunger and satisfy your longing. Amen.

Chapter 22

Giving It Up, Giving It *ALL* Up

Dealing with resentment

I am the good shepherd.... And I lay down my life for the sheep.... No one takes it from me, but I lay it down of my own accord.
John 10:14, 15, 18

When I graduated from college, I had every intention of pursuing a graduate or professional degree of some kind. I was newly married, living far away from anyone I knew, and wasn't exactly sure what direction I ought to take. Under the circumstances, I thought it would be best to take a year off from studies to adjust to my new station in life. I needed time to fully consider my options and goals. I began by collecting information and applications to various graduate programs in the area. I thought carefully, discerning and planning what I would do next. But six months later, when everything began to come into focus, I found out that I was pregnant.

Having a baby was not the next thing on my to do list at the time. Nonetheless, it was wonderfully exciting. The idea didn't upset my apple cart too much. After all, I had known plenty of graduate students who had completed their studies and had a baby too. It wouldn't be easy, but it wasn't impossible either. Nevertheless, I decided to put graduate school on hold until the baby was a year old.

Time flew by, and as our baby approached her first birthday, I began to pursue the further education I had tabled. But just as I was about to begin the first semester of classes, I conceived again. Needless to say, I was not a happy camper. I knew what it took to care for one child. I also knew that there was little chance of my being able to handle two children and a graduate education of any kind simultaneously. Although I wanted more than one child, I also wanted to go on with "my own" life. I felt as if all my aspirations were crashing down around me. I had to blame it on something, and the baby was the most logical choice.

As difficult as it was for me to adjust to having two children, it was even more difficult to stand by and watch my dreams die. I didn't have to worry any more about what kind of education or career to pursue. The answer was "none of the above." I didn't have to wonder whether I'd be happier as a lawyer or a professor, because I wouldn't be a lawyer or a professor. I was convinced that all I would be was what I already was—a mother. At the time, nothing could have been more discouraging. Whatever abilities I had would be buried under a pile of diapers. I felt like Gulliver, tied down and trapped by Lilliputians.

I really loved my two little girls. Yet underneath that love I nursed a great deal of resentment. Life wasn't turning out the way I had planned or prepared for, and I wasn't even twenty-five. I hadn't had time to accomplish much of anything and probably never would. I was envious of my husband's opportunity to develop his skills in the workplace. To make it worse, he was taking courses in a Master's program.

The demands of motherhood often make it difficult for a woman to achieve much in terms of her own personal development. I always get a laugh out of people who tell you to make sure that you have time for yourself. For me, in those early years, such moments weren't worth the backlog of falling behind in whatever had to be done. Usually by the time the children were in their beds, I was ready to crawl into mine.

Even when we really want to start a family, it can be difficult at times to resist feeling that our children somehow steal something from us. We all expect that raising children will cost us something in time, energy, and resources, but most of us idealize family life and tend to underestimate the sacrifices those glowing little faces ask of us. Family life is fulfilling, but in a different way from a hobby or even a job, because family life is a vocation, not just an occupation. It is something that takes up our lives not just our time.

Raising children is perhaps one of the most rewarding things we can do, but it isn't a walk down a garden path—it's challenging too. We can be fulfilled in family life when we hear the call to love and life and answer that call on a daily basis, yet the personal investment is enormous, and it stays that way over the long haul.

For me, the greatest challenge of family life is the same interior struggle we all face in trying to love others the way we love ourselves. At times that struggle can be a desperate one. Resentment can build up over time, and this bitterness can make us sour and grudging givers. It can become so deep that some of us attempt to live out our aspirations through the lives of our children. It can be so pervasive that we can use our children as an excuse; absolving ourselves from any real attempt to lead a productive life that may reach beyond the family.

Almost all of us await the day when our children are older and we can get back to making our own lives the priority. But that day never really comes because our children are not interruptions to our lives. They become the substance of our lives. I laugh when I think that the graduate degree I thought would be too difficult to try to work toward with two children, I am now pursuing (albeit slowly!) with eight.

We have all heard the saying, "small children—small problems; big children—big problems." From my point of view, I would replace the word "problems" with "sacrifices." Although we willingly make sacrifices for our children, we may hope and wish and think that someday the need to sacrifice will end. But if we take a look at our own lives, we may see that we ourselves necessitate sacrifices from those who love us. Indeed, as long as there is love there will be sacrifice. If we plan to love our children for the rest of our lives, then we must plan to sacrifice for the rest of our lives as well. And if we hope to love each other without limits, then we ought to be prepared to place no limits on what we are willing to give for one another.

The life of Mary is a portrait of loving well. In terms of self-sacrifice, Mary's Son was much more costly to her than most of our children are to us. If we really thought about it, few of us would want to trade places with her. By the end of her life on earth, Mary had given her all, beginning with her humanity to enflesh the Word of God and reaching its sacrificial summit as she stood beneath the cross. It ended with her surrendering herself into God's loving hands.

Like all of us, Mary was continually challenged to embrace greater and greater sacrifices. Mary's first yes was not her last. To be the mother of the Savior, Mary risked her reputation, her security, her privacy. She had to leave her home, her country, the rest of her family, and all of her plans behind. Whatever ideas she had about how she'd live her life took a back seat to God's plan of salvation. Indeed, Mary's whole identity would be overshadowed and defined by her divine Son. She gave everything for him, living her whole life for the sake of Christ. In the end, she gave him up to crowd and cross as well.

Mary's life was full of hardships, but it was also full of joy. In comparison with Mary, it seems that God asks so little of us. Why, then, do our lives of faith often seem lacking in joy? I think it is because when we sacrifice something, we often do it grudgingly. In trying to obey God's will, we may have agreed to let God take from us; but most of us have not yet learned how to give freely, with no strings attached and no expectation of return. There is little joy in letting someone take from us; but there is abundant joy in giving, especially in sacrificial giving. The Scriptures teach us that it was "for the sake of the joy that was set before him [he] endured the cross" (Heb 12:2).

The secret Mary knew was that God would exact nothing from her. The Lord would not take, but give. She also understood that she had the power to give her life to God or to hold it back entirely or in part. Choosing to lay down her whole life in love, Mary made herself a gift. That was the source of her joy.

Each of us possesses that very same power to give our lives to God. We know that no matter how much we give up for our children, somehow we always receive more in return. We know, too, that we cannot love our children well by giving them only our resources of time and money. We must give ourselves—our *whole* selves.

In our lives of discipleship, the same principle holds true. God will not be outdone in generosity. The

Lord gives us not just all of creation, but himself—the Creator—as well. The Father, Eternal Love, sacrifices not only all he has, but all he is in love for us. God keeps nothing of what we give to him, for whatever we sacrifice, whatever we give, serves only to multiply divine grace toward us. Most of what we long to cling to merely serves to keep us from God and, therefore, from our truest selves. What we sometimes struggle to grasp with our hands can steal the joy from our hearts.

O God, I treasure all your blessings. You have filled my life with good things to overflowing. You've given me all I have needed, and much of what I have desired. But Lord, I sometimes act as if your blessings are only meant for me—as if I am the sole beneficiary of your gifts. Though you have given to me without limits, I am often limiting what and how I give to others—even to those I love.

Lord, teach me to give without reservation, without counting the cost, without tabulating the return. Take away any resentment I may feel, and give me joy in its place. Teach me the art of sacrificial love. In every thing I give up, whether great or small, reveal to me the power of your redemption. Give me a true appreciation for the sacrifices others make. And inspire me to lay my life down as total gift; to give not only what I have, but what I am to your glory. Amen.

Chapter 23

The 24/7 Choice

Daycare and stay-at-home

The Lord will keep you from all evil;
he will keep your life.
The Lord will keep
your going out and your coming in
from this time on and forevermore.
Psalm 121:7–8

Several years ago, not long after the birth of our second child, I received a college alumni survey in the mail. The purpose of the form was to update the college community about what graduates had been doing. There were all kinds of boxes to check with pride: CEO, doctoral student, rabbi, research scientist, publisher, lawyer—everything you could imagine. Looking down the long list of professional activities, my heart sank. To me, it seemed that my life was amounting to very little. All I had done was give birth to a couple of children. All I was doing was staying home to take care of them.

I noticed, though, that there was a box for "housewife," and another one marked "taking time off to raise children." Looking around at the mess that is the natural byproduct of two children under two years of age, I decided to check both boxes. Obviously, I was taking time off from being a housewife in order to raise children!

That survey prompted a moment of embarrassment and shame. It seemed to me that I had done very little with my very prestigious college education. I was sure that others would draw the same conclusion. The strange thing was that while I couldn't claim any big professional position or success, I felt completely challenged—even overwhelmed—by what it took to be a "stay-at-home" mother. My "work" was every bit as demanding as any of those other occupations. It just didn't come with paychecks, letters of commendation, or promotions of any kind. In the end I decided not to return the survey.

For the most part, I've left work outside the home to others. Since graduating from college, I have never held a full-time job. I think, though, that if that same alumni survey was sent to me today, I would check off a lot more boxes: health care provider, educator, child psychologist, human resource manager, communications director, food services worker, travel and entertainment coordinator, and time resource manager.

Raising eight children has thrust me into just about every conceivable discipline in one way or another. On any given day, I am working in many fields. I'd check off those boxes now not because I am actually doing more than I did then, but because I have learned to see what I'm doing as a mother in a different light.

While I've sometimes looked with envy at women who are well-paid and respected professionals, I have met many who wished that they were able to do what I'm doing. Their struggle is different from mine, but it is a struggle nonetheless.

For a mother who works outside the home, living in two very different worlds can be disorienting. The stress of trying to mesh and balance the demands of family and work can make a women feel like she can't win in either sphere. Women who plan to continue their pursuit of career goals face difficult choices about who will care for their children while they are working. Many also find themselves dealing with a sense of guilt or uncertainty regarding those choices or the way their choices are viewed by others.

The reality is that all of us need and do some kind of work. And all of us need and have some kind of home. Work gives us a vehicle for self-expression and the dignity of being productive. Home is the place where we have the freedom to be truly ourselves and genuinely with others. The challenge for women today is to resist compartmentalizing our lives into boxes. Instead, we can pioneer creative ways to allow the whole of our lives to encompass all we do in both task and relationship.

For me, that has meant pursuing most of my professional goals from home. This book, for example, has been written largely in my kitchen between the endless interruptions that emanate from pre-school children during the day. My schedule outside the home is entirely up to me. Each family member's calendar is influenced by every other, and conflicts are addressed as a whole family team. While I know that not every kind of work can be done in this way, I've been able to find adequate outlets for my abilities and interests while remaining faithful to my responsibilities as a mother of eight. Rather than having a "professional" me in one place and a "mommy" me in another, integrating work with family life has helped me be more of who I am at all times. I've also had the comfort of knowing that even when I am "at work," I am also available "at home."

For others, who work outside the home, integrating work with family life takes another shape. Finding safe and reliable daycare, accommodating after-school friendships, shouldering one's share of a carpool, helping with homework after a long day, leaving work to pick up a sick child…these and more can leave a woman feeling frazzled and fragmented. Finding a way to balance the demands of working outside the home with the primary responsibility of mothering is not easy, but it is a challenge that cannot be sidestepped. While there are full-time and part-time job opportunities, there is no such thing as a part-time mother.

In the same vein it must be said that every mother is a working woman. Whatever we do between nine and five, motherhood is not a job or a career. It is a vocation of self-giving that is always open. Every mother, in and outside the home, is a mother twenty-five hours a day.

The choices we make about how we use our time and other resources do have an impact on everyone in a household. But my children don't care how many books I write, or how many people hear me speak. They don't care much either if I have managed to get rid of the most stubborn stains in the shower tile grout. To them, I'm just "Mom."

Mary didn't have a career or much of a resume. Few of us, however, have lived our lives to their fullest potential as much as she. Mary became all she was capable of becoming. She achieved (if we can use that term when speaking of her) far more than most of us.

The secret of Mary's exemplary life, I think, is that she did what was *at hand.* I can't imagine her complaining about what was not available to her. I can't picture her romanticizing someone else's life either. I suspect Mary spent very little time thinking about where the grass might be greener. Instead, she got out there and mowed her own lawn. Mary fulfilled her every responsibility. In doing so, she grew to her full stature as a woman of God.

Mary's life shows us the link between caring *about* and caring *for* someone. Because God was at the heart of Mary's concern, she made caring for Jesus her life's work. She did so knowing that God cared about her enough to care for her as well. There is a bond which is forged by filling simple and daily needs. I think that is why Jesus taught us to ask our heavenly Father for daily bread. God longs to share such a bond with us.

The needs and wants of others present us with countless opportunities for loving service. None of us can single-handedly meet every need our children will have. But our responsibility as parents is to assure that their needs will, in some way, be met. No matter if we're home 24/7 or working eight hours a day, the bread that nourishes family life is the caring and concern we show each other every day.

O God, you care for me and about me. You are always there for me, and you are attentive to my every need and desire. More than anything, you want me to spend time just being with you. But Lord, sometimes I'm too busy for my own good. I try to balance everything, but there are days when even the scale can't hold the weight of it all. In all the things I have to do, I lose sight of who I am and of who you are as well. The days go speeding by.

Help me to see the gift of every moment, and to answer the call of others' needs. Give me wisdom in how to live my life, not just in the big choices I make on occasion, but in the thousands of little ones I make every day. Teach me to live within my means: within the limitations of my own life as it really is. Give me joy in faithfulness and in simple things well done. And help me to find your presence in doing what you have set before me. Amen.

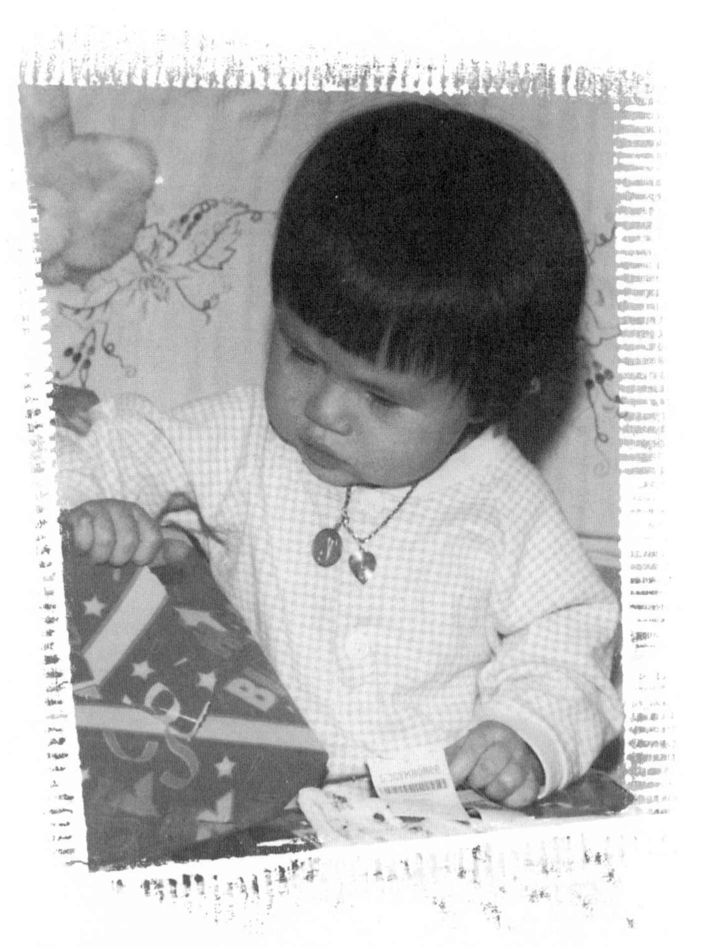

Chapter 24

When the Thrill Is Gone

Boredom and exhaustion

"Come to me, all you that are weary and are carrying heavy burdens, and I will give you rest. Take my yoke upon you, and learn from me; for I am gentle and humble in heart, and you will find rest for your souls. For my yoke is easy, and my burden is light."
Matthew 11:28–30

Every pregnancy begins with a great deal of excitement. Regardless of whether a woman is expecting her first child or her eighth, new life gives us a thrill. It is like taking a walk in a spring garden at the end of a long winter. There may be nothing new to us about daffodils or tulips, but we find the garden fresh and lovely nonetheless.

Pregnancy was never a secret I could keep. Although there were times that I thought it would be best to delay any announcements, it was never long before I'd be on the phone telling everyone the good news. Like a little girl, I played maternity dress-up. And I delighted in filling the dresser drawers with little undershirts and tiny socks.

I noticed that my husband smiled more when I was pregnant. It was almost as if he knew something I didn't. But he wasn't the only one who got into the act. Our kids have relished accompanying me to doctor visits. They loved to hear the pure magic of a new baby's heartbeat. I have to admit that I even pulled four of them out of school so they could "meet" their youngest brother on ultrasound. For our kids—especially the girls—maternity has been as delicious as a hot fudge sundae. The whole thing opened up a completely new realm of fantasy for them. I remember when they were little, our oldest girls played mommy by stuffing dolls under their dresses. For our sons, the experience has been mysterious and strange—the kind of thing that makes little boys giggle and run out of the room.

It has surprised me that even when I would have rather not been expecting another child, excitement has still been part of every pregnancy. In the early weeks, I have always felt like I was walking on air. It was a sensation very much like falling in love. I suppose, in fact, that is what it is: falling in love with a new child. The morning sickness, the weight gain, the exhaustion—none of that seemed as important as the new baby that was coming! A uniquely new person was on the way!

But as the weeks and months passed, that romantic air grew stale. Just getting around became a major production. I could hardly fit behind the driver's wheel, let alone fasten a seat belt. My feet and ankles swelled so much that I found it difficult to walk. The days were full of backaches and heartburn, while restless nights were punctuated by frequent trips to the bathroom. Over the years I have developed an extensive maternity wardrobe with lots of things for every season and occasion. Nevertheless, I always felt like I had nothing to wear. (I can't imagine why I ever thought those big white collars were cute!) And to top it off, during five of my pregnancies I broke out in an itchy rash that would drive anyone crazy. Suffice it to say that in every instance of maternity, I eventually got sick and tired of being sick and tired—and my family did, too.

There comes a time in every pregnancy when nothing seems worth the effort; when maternity becomes a "gift" we'd like to return or exchange. Most of us would agree that pregnancy and children are a lot of fun. But when we are exhausted, or at the end of our rope, suddenly the fun is over. The excitement dies down just as the hard work of pregnancy gets harder. Our wonder at the miracle of it all wears very thin. Eventually, the things that were once a source of joy become a burden.

Interestingly, there is a certain one-upmanship among women regarding childbearing and children. I think of the many times I've heard the horrors of pregnancy and birth from one woman, just to hear another in her company trump her with something even worse. I usually wait until everyone is finished singing the woes of delivering an eight or nine pound infant, then I chime in with my eleven and a half pounder. These are the feminine equivalents of war stories or, in some cases, fish stories. The accounts of our sufferings serve as our medals of honor. The more difficult our circumstances, the greater our claim is to maternal glory.

Exaggerating our sacrifices and minimizing our blessings, however, produces an exasperated heart. Focusing on the difficulties we face over the long haul make it easier for them to overshadow and sour us. Because pregnancy is naturally self-absorbing, it doesn't take much for us to slip beyond that into self-centeredness. Self-centeredness can then spill into our relationships with our children.

While we love our children, we can sometimes try every available means to get out from under them. We can't wait until that baby is born, or until he's in bed for the night, or until school begins again. Under the yoke of what we must bear, we can be tempted to view not only the struggles of pregnancy, but pregnancy itself—and even our children—as merely burdensome.

Mary didn't have it any easier than the vast majority of us. As awesome as it must have been to be the mother of the Messiah, the reality was far from fairytale glamour. It involved all the hardships of ordinary life and then some. I think, if she had wanted to, Mary could have told many "war stories" about the struggles she faced. Yet, the Scriptures do not contain the agonies of Mary's trials. Rather, they record her joys, and the glory of God's blessings.

The immense responsibility given to Mary as the mother of Jesus taught her to rely on God for strength. As weak as she found herself to be, she knew that God was strong. As heavy as the burden became, she believed that she could trust the Lord to carry her through it. With each new obstacle, God showed Mary how much he loved her in a new way. Although the difficulties she faced were very real, Mary knew that the glory of God was just as real, perhaps even more real, because it would endure forever. Her soul was able to proclaim the greatness of God because her spirit found joy in God himself.

Just as we sometimes lose our sense of joy and wonder in childbearing, we also lose joy in our lives of faith. We may start with a fire of love and exuberance. But as the years pass, we are sometimes lucky to end up with even a spark. It is hard to avoid being inundated by drudgery of the spirit. It is possible to count the cost of discipleship so much that we forget who paid the bill in the first place. If we make too much of our own sacrifices, we can lose sight of the One who sacrificed everything for us. Faith can become burdensome to us. I see this in myself when I begin to talk a great deal about "crosses," but not very much about the cross of Christ. In those times, I have acted as if it is God who demands that I carry a heavy load. I plod along, bowing low under the crushing weight of faithfulness. That is when I get the inkling that there is something wrong.

Discipleship is not meant to be a joyless existence, but a joyful life. Indeed, life can be heavy and burdensome. But the giver of life and eternal life does not abandon us to our own weakness. The Scriptures teach us that his "power is made perfect in weakness" (2 Cor 12:9), and that "the joy of the Lord is [our] strength" (Neh 8:10).

When life weighs us down, Jesus invites us to come to him. He promises to refresh our souls. Even though in the cross he carries the weight of the sins of the world, he tells us that his "yoke is easy, and [his] burden is light" (Mt 11:30), because in comparison to the joy of salvation, the great pains he endured were as nothing. If, like Mary, we take his yoke upon ourselves and learn from him, we would see his presence in our lives as the pure gift of grace. There is no greater thrill. If we could cultivate hearts like the heart of Jesus—full of gentleness and humility—perhaps we also would call our burdens light.

O Lord, when I first heard your call, it rang like music in my ears. When I first began to walk with you, my steps were quick and sure. My heart blossomed with newfound love. My spirit was giddy with joy.

But somewhere along the way, Lord, I grew tired. The sound of your voice became too familiar. My feet began to ache from the long and difficult road. My heart became preoccupied and my soul weighed down.

Restore to me, O God, the sweetness of that first taste of you. Rekindle in me a new fire of devotion, and reawaken in me a passion for your presence. Help me to discern your call in the lives of others. Teach me the love that bears all things, that makes all things new, that calls all burdens light. Give me a gentle and humble heart that I might find strength in your joy. Amen.

Chapter 25

Waiting

Building patience

For you I wait all day long.
Psalm 25:5

As I get older, I have come to the conclusion that time flies whether you're having fun or not. It seems that each year passes more quickly than the last; that Christmas comes on the heels of the Fourth of July, and that children grow up far too fast for their own good—or mine. Life roars past at such a pace that we hardly have time to catch our breath. Almost everything feels like an "all of a sudden."

Pregnancy, however, has a clock all its own. It's puzzling how in some ways forty weeks can seem like forty days, and in others like forty years. Acquaintances always appear to have children in record time, while friends and relatives move steadily along the course. But what I could never understand is why everyone else's pregnancies were over and done with quickly, and mine seemed to go on forever!

In the great scheme of things, nine months is a drop in the bucket of eternity. Nonetheless, while we are pregnant, nine months can feel a lot like eternity. After the initial excitement wears off, maternity begins to resemble the forty years of wandering in the desert. We have the sense that we are going nowhere fast, or just wasting time walking around in circles. Frustration makes it easy to doubt whether or not a promised land even exists.

Other people often contribute to our growing impatience with their own. All of our children, when expecting a new brother or sister, constantly flipped the kitchen calendar back and forth counting the weeks until the due date. Most of our conversation circled around the new baby, and whether I thought he would be early or late. I never quite understood why anyone thought that the topic was even relevant, as babies three through six were all induced about one week before due. My husband the computer expert was always prepared to calculate the number of hours until the projected birth. The whole thing was much like the stereotypical family car vacation. Everything echoed with incessant "are-we-there-yets?"

Waiting is never easy. When there's something to look forward to, or something we wish would end, we even say, "I just can't wait." Yet wait we must, because for most of us a great deal of life is spent waiting. Whether we can or not is immaterial. Waiting is something we all must do. It is the emotional equivalent of death and taxes.

In our "ten items or less" world of instant gratification, we have lost the ability to wait well. Rather than embrace the natural rhythms of life, I think many of us have thought it both possible and preferable to make our lives a continual feast. A lot of us have exempted ourselves from fasting of any kind. We've fallen into considering such things arcane, unnecessary, and undesirable. Because it is hard to see the value of doing without, we refuse hunger. But in so doing, we also refuse what hunger can teach us. We diminish not only the purpose, but the joy of the feast. We can end up acting more like gluttonous consumers than grateful guests.

For me, the long weeks of pregnancy are the fast before the feast, the lenten desert before the Easter of new life. As aggravating as waiting is, it sets the stage for the great joy that accompanies birth. The longing, wonder, and anticipation that dominates—and irritates—us is what makes the experience of childbearing so happy. It is the emptiness that makes us capable of being filled, and the thirst that allows us to be satisfied.

When I think of Mary waiting for the birth of her Son, I see the whole world waiting silently and unknowingly with her. The aspirations and longings of all human history are contained in those forty weeks of her life. For, from the beginning, people of every nation have sought the Divine Presence. After Christ himself, the expectant Virgin Mary is both the crown and summation of all humanity. She is the expression of all souls hungering for their Creator, awaiting his promised redemption. It was not for a mere nine months that the world awaited the birth of Christ, but for all time.

In my own life, I have found it much easier to wait for a new baby than to wait for God. At least we know that all pregnancies do, in fact, come to an end. But sometimes in our spiritual lives, there seems to be no end to the waiting we must endure. It is easy to become impatient with God. We grumble like the children of Israel in the desert who wondered why Yahweh did not bring them to the fullness of his promise without delay.

It is understandable to fear that when we need the Lord, he may not come. Or that if he does, it will be too late. But the fullness of the promise only comes in the fullness of time. Our God is the Lord of the eleventh hour, fifty-ninth minute, and fifty-ninth second. God lives in the "nick of time," and in the breath between the prayer we pray and the amen—or so be it—at the end.

The irony of pregnancy is that all our impatience comes from waiting for someone who is already there, with us and within us. Similarly, the mystery of our faith is that we await the coming of a God who is already here and always near to us. The Lord never loses patience with us; the fire of God's passion for us never dies down. God is always coming to us, but we are not always ready or able to receive the Spirit.

Waiting in faith is more than spiritual thumb-twiddling. It is the fuel for the hope and desire that burns in our souls. Waiting centers our attention on whatever it is we are waiting for. We need to wait, because while God is always focused on us, we aren't always fixed on God. Our Lord gives our hearts time to ripen. The Master knows that every apple picked too soon will be sour.

Ripening time can seem to last forever. Many of us, at least on occasion, have felt as if we have waited a lifetime for God to answer a prayer or make himself known to us. It is like waiting to hear the final note of a symphony, or watching a football game in which the last two minutes of play last half an hour. We grow exasperated waiting our turn. Our faith burns down like candles on an Advent wreath lit week after week. Sometimes struggling to keep the vigil, we lose hope that God will ever have time for us.

Beyond time, however, there is Someone else who waits. From all eternity, the Holy One has waited for each one of us to turn to him. For all eternity, the Father waits for us to embrace him with our whole hearts. The One who was, who is, who is to come, has already come to us. Yet, until we come to God, Advent never ends—and Christmas comes only in the hearts of those who attend to God's presence.

O Lord, you pursue my soul like a passionate lover. You are always at my heels, not even a step behind me. You are close enough to hear the whispers of my heart. You have fixed your attention on me forever.

Yet, when I turn to reach for you, you seem to vanish, Lord. You become a master of hesitation and delay. Your voice is silent and your touch withdrawn. My soul searches for you and does not find you. I wait impatiently for you to come, and wonder if you will ever arrive.

Lord, remind me that it is not I, but you, who wait. Teach me to trust in you and to wait well. Help me to be patient with myself and with others. Show me how to center my whole being on you, O God. And teach me to live in this day, but not for it. Rather, set my heart on what is eternal, and ripen my soul for your harvest. Amen.

Chapter 26

Expecting and Expectations

Managing our agendas

> Then the mother of the sons of Zebedee came to him with her sons, and kneeling before him, she asked a favor of him. . . . "Declare that these two sons of mine will sit, one at your right hand and one at your left, in your kingdom."
>
> Matthew 20:20, 21

Music has always been an important part of my life. Naturally, I planned on sharing it with my children. Although I had studied several musical instruments, I had always wanted to try the harp. When I found myself expecting our first child, I thought about how wonderful it would be if that child could learn to play the harp. In fact, I did more than just think about it. I bought several recordings of harp music and systematically played at least one of them every day. I even "piped them in" by occasionally putting headphones on my stomach! Thankfully, I didn't have the time to pursue such foolishness with our second and successive children.

When our girls got older, I asked them to think carefully about which instrument they might like to play. If it suited their ability and our budget, we would go along with it. Without any hesitation our second daughter came up with the flute. And, to my delight, our oldest said she was interested in the harp! I couldn't believe it had actually worked!

Sadly, however, we quickly discovered that the harp was far too expensive. The instrument itself could be rented, but the instruction alone was three times more costly than other instruments. Moreover, instructors were few and far between, and most of them weren't interested in teaching a seven year old. The harp was simply not in our cards—even though I had stacked the deck. Instead, our oldest girl pursued ballet with a passion, and our second is still playing her flute. The others have done all kinds of things: fencing, step dancing, trumpet, piano, scouting—you name it. The wonderful thing is that the desire to do these activities came from them.

Expectations are never in short supply. Most first-time mothers anticipate leaving the hospital in their pre-pregnancy clothes. (I was even silly enough to pack mine the first two times through.) Similarly, we have definite ideas of how our babies are "supposed to" develop: sit by six months, crawl by nine, walk by twelve. But these expectations can entrap us. Many a mother has sheepishly apologized for children who don't "measure up" in these often arbitrary ways. I know how embarrassed I was with our oldest son, who refused to say anything intelligible until he was nearly three. I had two more children who were slow to speak; now, they hardly stop talking!

We live most of life somewhere in the gap between what is real and what is ideal. Things do not always turn out the way we think or hope they will. Part of growing wiser is being able to distinguish between hopes and expectations. Hopes inspire, direct, and guide. They are freely and unconditionally given. Expectations inhibit, control, and bind. They may masquerade as hopes, but they come with strings attached. All mothers have hopes both for themselves and for their children. But if we allow these hopes to become expectations, we set ourselves and our children up for a lot of disappointment.

Parental expectations often reflect parental concerns and even fears. As our children grow, our expectations change, but they do not disappear. Potty training soon gives way to ABCs, reading, math, and report cards. Climbing the stairs is replaced by little league and dance recitals. Eventually, all the things of childhood evolve into concerns about education, jobs, marriages, and grandchildren. Those concerns also embrace things that are every parent's worst nightmare: alcohol and drug abuse, sexual immorality, and general irresponsibility.

However we choose to define "perfect," most of us want "perfect" children. There is no such thing as an impartial parent. (Nor should there be!) We all believe that *our* children are better than everyone else's. In truth, I think every child needs someone in his or her life who truly believes that he is the best. But there are ways in which we may cross into demanding that they be so, and at all times.

In the process of doing all we can for our children, the line between the hopes we have had for ourselves and those we have for our children can become blurred. Loving our children, we want them to succeed. We want to keep them from making our mistakes. We hope that they will do more than we did, and become more than we are. But sometimes it is hard to resist looking to them to fulfill some of the dreams we have laid aside. We begin to expect something *from* them. When that happens, we stop giving ourselves to our children freely. Instead, we begin investing ourselves in them with an eye toward some kind of return.

At an even deeper level, parental agendas can interfere with the unconditional love our children need. Regardless of what they are, our expectations orient our children toward ourselves. More often they serve as obstacles to our approval than as tools of personal development. Moreover, such expectations elevate the importance of our pride, sometimes at the expense of God's glory. I could certainly muster the force of will to push my children into almost anything. But at what cost? What desires of theirs, and even more importantly, what divine purposes would be squelched in the process? That rather self-directed love makes our children exclusively ours. Unconditional love makes them free to be and become who they are for themselves, for the world, and for the God who made them in the first place.

When Mary took her part in God's plan of salvation, she gave up not only the expectations she had for herself, but also those for the divine child she would bear. No doubt, as the mother of Jesus, Mary possessed tremendous influence over her Son. She was his first teacher. Nonetheless, it appears that Mary did not push her own agenda either on her Son or on God. She made herself the handmaid of the Lord. She did not seek to define or influence the divine purpose, but to serve it.

Whatever her ideas might have been, Mary surrendered them to the plan God had in mind. Rather than having hopes *for* her Son, she chose to place her hopes *in* him. The truth is that, like all of us, Mary did not know what to expect—only whom. She could not anticipate the events of her life, either good or bad. She did not know what time would reveal. Expecting Jesus, Mary expected the movement of God for salvation. It wasn't any more specific than that. She held on to the promise, and let go of everything else.

Letting go, however, does not mean distancing ourselves from our children. Rather, it is surrendering our claims of ownership over them, and placing their lives into both their hands and God's. I think that Joseph is the clearest example of letting go without drawing back. Without a doubt, Mary's baby threw a wrench in the works of just about all of Joseph's expectations. Engaged to a virgin, Joseph suddenly found himself in strange and deep waters.

Instead of turning his back on Mary and her child, Joseph drew nearer to them both. For their sake, he embraced the unknown and mysterious will of God and accepted the challenging ways of God. In that moment, Joseph not only welcomed God's child as his own, but in place of his own. Rather than agonizing over unfulfilled expectations, Joseph responded in faith. He risked believing that God would give him more, and not less. In the end, he was not disappointed.

Mary and Joseph teach us that the need to let go of our expectations begins even before our babies are born. In reality, our children are not only ours, they belong, as we all do, to God. It is God who entrusts them to our care for a time.

The Heavenly Father, however, not only trusts us with the care of our children's needs, he gives us their potential as well. As parents, we are responsible for developing our children's abilities as fully as we can. For while our children are children, God's purpose for them is left in our hands. The excellence of our parenting is perhaps best measured by how much our children progress in accomplishing God's plans—and not ours or theirs—for their lives. There will certainly be times of setback and even failure. We instruct them best, I think, by following God's will ourselves.

As disciples of Jesus, each of us is entrusted with the spiritual potential we posses in faith. Most of us spend lots of time trying to discern what our gifts are and how to develop them. Unfortunately, many of us retreat into labels of faith. We characterize ourselves as "traditional" or "charismatic," "active" or "contemplative." But in defining ourselves in these ways, we box our souls into predetermined spiritual practices.

Allowing wherever we are at any point in time to evolve into spiritual expectations interferes with God's desire to lead us deeper. When we narrow the spectrum of how we will allow God to move in us, we anticipate more and participate less. We train our spirits to expect things *from* God, but not necessarily God *himself*. And when we don't get what we expect, or receive it in the way we expected, we can be disappointed.

If we were able to allow God's hopes to take precedence over our own expectations, we would never be disappointed. Our Lord's hopes for us are far beyond what we could hope for ourselves. If we could learn to distance ourselves from our *selves*, we would be closer to God. Jesus taught us that if we would only seek God's kingdom first, we would have everything else besides (cf. Mt 6:33). How much happier we would be if, learning to let go of other things, we could learn to cling to God alone.

O Lord, with you all things are possible! You walk on water, you heal the sick, you even raise the dead. You give hope to the distressed; no one who hopes in you is disappointed. Yet Lord, sometimes I have been disappointed. For there are times when you seem slow to answer me; when you lead me down paths that I don't want to take, times when I've seen my dreams shattered around me.

Deliver me, O God, from expecting things and teach me to expect you instead. Keep me from plans and ideas that are mine, but not yours. Help me to embrace your hopes as my own. Teach me to see your purpose in the lives of others and to do what I can to help them fulfill it. Give me a faith that surrenders my claims to anything but you. Remind me that I am your servant, and not your advisor. And make me a handmaid of your perfect will. Amen.

Chapter 27

The Not-So-Blessed Event

Postpartum depression

"And God will wipe away every tear from their eyes."

Revelation 7:17

Joy is an unquestionable part of childbearing, but so is stress. There's no getting around the fact that motherhood can be overwhelming in every way. Physically, maternity pushes us to every limit of strength and energy. Emotionally, we can find ourselves lost in a maze of mixed feelings so intense that we can hardly keep ourselves from acting out of psychological vertigo. Spiritually, motherhood opens new vistas of God's work in and through us. At times this can include dark and unknown pathways of growth that can be frightening and disconcerting.

Every new mother, even if she has had several children, is awash in the ocean of her own bodily chemistry and the tides of her day to day responsibilities. At one time or another, we have all been victims of our own hormones, schedules, or "to do" lists. It takes time—sometimes several months—for us to get back in the swing of things. I remember totally falling apart in a grocery store when our second child was about six months old. Suddenly, and for no apparent reason, I was overcome with panic. I had lost sight of my husband, who was pushing a cart with one of our children in it. My response was completely instinctive and uncontrollable. I shouted out quite loudly in the middle of the store, and burst into tears. It took several minutes for me to calm down.

I made an appointment with my obstetrician to discuss what had happened. His diagnosis wasn't exactly medical. As he put it, I was twenty-five, not a millionaire, and under considerable stress as the mother of two young children. He advised me to eat more frequently, cut back on caffeine, and avoid unnecessary stress, especially in the afternoons. Knowing that I couldn't realistically do any of those things, I just about broke down and cried. Eventually, he prescribed medication to regulate my hormones. After a while, I returned to normal. Sometimes I wonder what life would have been like if things didn't get any better.

Unfortunately, some of us don't have to wonder. Postpartum depression is very real. Just at what is supposed to be the happiest time of her life, a woman in postpartum depression may feel almost nothing. While everyone around her is buzzing, she can't share the joy. She may be plagued with inescapable sadness, or feel nervous and anxiety ridden. Whatever she feels is compounded by guilt over being sad at all. All the "shoulds" make it difficult to accept the way things really are. She may wonder, too, if she is capable of caring adequately for her children.

Postpartum depression is not the same as the natural let down most of us feel after the emotionally intense birth experience. The "baby blues" usually come a few days after birth, and pass just as quickly. But when symptoms last more than two weeks, we may be suffering from something more serious. Women can experience the onset of postpartum depression within a few days of delivery or more gradually—even up to a year later. Untreated, postpartum depression can last a considerable time.

Perhaps the most difficult symptoms of postpartum depression are feelings of inadequacy and hopelessness. The truth is that women who are clinically depressed after birth are being treated in a variety of ways and with great success. While most of us wouldn't think twice about going to the doctor for any other illness, many of us fear that postpartum depression reflects badly on us as mothers. Yet, there is no need to be ashamed of any unanticipated illness. The most important thing is to ask for help whenever you need it.

It may be comforting for every woman to know that Mary probably had down days too. Like every other woman, the mother of Jesus bore the stresses and uncertainties of motherhood. I would imagine there were times when Mary doubted her adequacy for the great task ahead of her, times when she felt overwhelmed, or exhausted, or sad. Mary's life was not a bouquet of roses without thorns. She faced all the realities of human life. She worked and struggled. She mothered her child the same way we do, with no magic tricks or miracles up her sleeves. Mary was only human.

When we are down and out, we can turn to Mary. Sharing our pain and embarrassment, we can find in her a wise and gentle friend. Mary understands because she has walked the same challenging road we're on. She can give us counsel and support because she has been there herself. She can guide and direct us because she has finished the course. Even more, she can give us her prayers. When we are too tired to pray, too disillusioned to hope, too afraid to try again, Mary is there, as is God. When we feel more like children than like mothers, Mary consoles us.

While the communion of angels and saints is not a substitute for medical care, it is a great well from which all of us can draw spiritual assistance. The angels show us the glory of God. The saints show us God's faithfulness. Whatever difficulties we encounter in life, there was some faithful disciple in history who faced and overcame it by grace. That very same healing grace is ours for the asking, because the very same God who gave it to them is our Father as well.

O Lord, you have given me everything I need to be happy. You have surrounded me with joyful singing. You have held me close. But there are times when I am inexplicably sad; when I cannot see or smell or taste your goodness; days when I close in upon myself and wonder if I will ever be happy again.

Lord, save me from my fears and give me hope. Teach me that when I call for help you will always answer. Keep me from the shame that sometimes encircles my heart and the guilt which can paralyze me. Help me to be aware of what others bear, and touch me with your healing grace. Amen.

Chapter 28

Making Your Mess and Cleaning It Too!

Admitting our own imperfections

"Be perfect, therefore, as your heavenly Father is perfect."

Matthew 5:48

Before I had children, I didn't think much about how to raise them. But when we began having a family, it seemed as if we could think of little else. I remember having plenty of discussions with my husband about parenting, especially regarding discipline. But in those early years of inexperience, it was all trial and error—and believe me, it had more error than anything else.

As much as I wanted perfect children, I wanted even more to be a perfect mother. I remember the terror I felt during that first drive home from the hospital. I wondered what in the world I was supposed to do with this baby? Was it really a question of following natural maternal instincts? The talk shows were full of countless stories of mothers who had scarred their children for life. Obviously, they had done something wrong. But I wasn't sure how to avoid it, because I couldn't really be sure what it was about.

I supposed you could judge the tree by its fruit. Obviously "bad" mothers produced "bad"—or badly damaged—children. But there were too many examples to the contrary of wonderful parents and families who somehow ended up with troubled adult children. It seemed to me that by the time you figured out what you were doing right or wrong, it would be too late.

To me, the greatest challenge of child raising was, and is, discipline. Being a hot-tempered person with high standards for child behavior, I tend to lose patience with young children. Sometimes my expectations of them have been simply off the mark. Other times, my ideas of how best to deal with a situation got me into a bind. I remember one incident in particular with our second, very strong-willed daughter. I had already warned, yelled, and sent her to her room. I had no alternatives left. Still defiant, I told her that if she didn't stop, I would throw her out the window. Of course I didn't mean it, and she knew it. We ended in a stalemate.

Not knowing where to turn at times, I concluded that perhaps the best way to learn good mothering was to watch other women doing it. I saw parents who were more strict and those who were more lenient that I had been. I noticed some who were highly-interventionist, and others who were more laissez-faire. I observed women talking calmly to their seriously misbehaving children, never raising their voices and never coming anywhere close to spanking them. In contrast, I remembered in my own upbringing a good deal of hollering and a few spanks when I was particularly disobedient. Seeing the range of techniques and results highlighted for me how large the acceptable parenting spectrum is between the unacceptable extremes of abuse and neglect. The whole "study" was inconclusive as both the subjects and the results were very mixed.

Next, I tried the textbook approach. At the suggestion of some friends who were at a loss themselves, I resorted to some of the methods and techniques suggested by parenting "experts." I remember debating which chair I would designate as the "time out chair," and getting together the various materials I would need as if I was setting up some sort of laboratory. The one thing I never did figure out was which one of us was the guinea pig in the experiment!

Invariably, every book stressed the importance of consistency with children. That turned out to be my problem with every technique. As hard as I tried, I could not maintain consistency in any of these methods. I just couldn't keep up the front of acting like someone I wasn't. Frustrated and exhausted, I threw up my hands and rolled up my sleeves.

It finally occurred to me that as much as my own weaknesses got in the way of my being a good mother, pretending they weren't there or trying to eliminate them all at once made things even worse. The fact is that *I* was the mother of my children. To be sure, I have my share of faults and limitations, but so do my children. So, indeed, does everybody. The quality of my mothering was not dependent on how many books I had read or which expert advice I chose to follow. It depended on what kind of a person I was and was becoming.

Things got much better when I recognized that despite all the advice I could gather, and regardless of how hard I tried, I was going to make mistakes as a mother. Both my children and I would suffer the consequences of those mistakes, but we could also learn from them. Over the years I have changed how I mother my children. I'm more patient that I used to be, but sometimes less energetically involved too. I know that there are times I have fallen woefully short. Like everyone else, I have to live with things I regret having said or done out of my own deficiencies. But I am still trying to get it right, and to make it right when I've been wrong.

As the mother of Jesus, Mary must have been continually aware of her limitations. She was, after all, a young and inexperienced mother. I'm sure too, that Mary had her share of challenges in raising her Son.

She must have felt the weight of the enormous responsibility she had. If she "failed" as a mother, there was no telling what dreadful consequences would follow.

There were no child development experts in ancient Israel. The only expert advice Mary would have would come from the women in her village, and any guidance her own mother might give. And when circumstances forced the Holy Family to depart for Egypt, she left all of them behind. In a land of strangers, Mary—like the rest of us—had to find herself and her own way.

Aware of both the importance of her task and her own limitations, Mary did not live out her life's mission in fear and anxiety. Rather, she approached her work as she did God, with confidence—that is, with faith. Mary knew there was no mask to hide behind that God could not see through. She didn't try to be someone "better" or "wiser" or "stronger" than she was. It was not because she believed in herself, but because she believed in God. Whether or not there was someone better or wiser or stronger for the job, the Lord had chosen her.

We all experience times when the only things we can be certain of are our own inadequacies. In those periods, we can be afraid of what others may think, and then resort to masking who we really are. Not even realizing what we are doing, we hide behind pretense to protect ourselves from "failure." We act out our lives rather than live them. Like important papers stashed in a special place for safe keeping, we put our true selves away. But when we need them, it is easy to forget where it was we put them.

As hard as it is to be someone other than who we are in the presence of others, it is even harder to do it in the presence of God. Nonetheless, from time to time many of us attempt to do exactly that. Afraid to be our poor selves with God, we put on all the "holy" things we think the Almighty wants of us. We come to God with all the perfection we can muster. We even design elaborate methods to reach God. But the truth is that the life of faith must be mothered, not engineered. There are no high-tech highways to heaven.

God has little use for our spiritual techniques or fig leaves. Our Heavenly Father does not want us to hide ourselves in false piety or feigned "holiness." What pleases God is faith, pure and simple—even *im*pure and simple. God teaches us that we do not need faith in our strength and holiness, but in God's loving mercy toward both our infirmity and our infidelity. Through this faith the Holy One gives us hope that someday "we shall be like him, for we shall see him as he is" (1 Jn 3:2).

O Lord, you are a holy God. You are perfect wisdom, gentle strength, and unbridled love. What is there in me for you to desire? Yet, you created me in your image to reflect your glory.

Lord, how can I come to you as I am? For your shallows are too deep for me. Before your gentleness I am weak, and by the light of your love I see the poverty of my own.

Help me to approach you without fear, O God. Strip away any pretense or falsity from my soul. Center my faith in your mercy, Lord, and not in my own works or worth. Teach me to be myself in the presence of others and to affirm who others truly are. Teach me to accept those you choose, even when they are not my choice. For now, Lord, hide me beneath your wings. But one day, show me your face and make me like yourself. Amen.

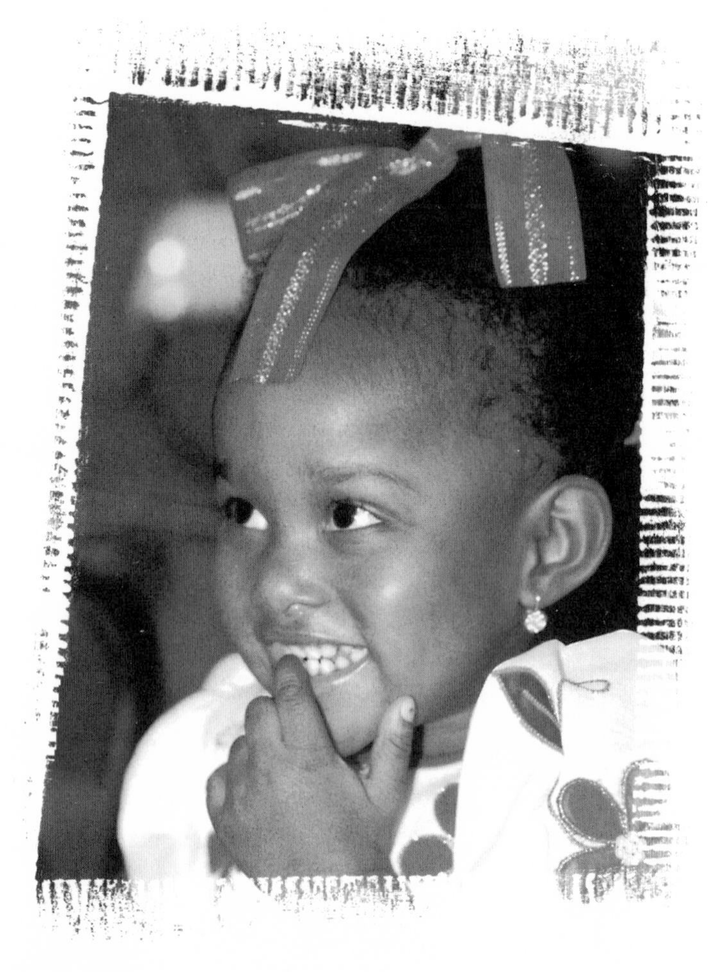

Chapter 29

The Love Gap

Recognizing that we are not enough

"This is my commandment, that you love one another as I have loved you."
John 15:12

A day or two after our first child was born, I sat down in my hospital room to make a list of the things the baby would need. I already had all the big items, but in no time at all the paper was filled. Diapers, undershirts, sleepers, socks, baby powder, pacifiers, shampoo, hooded towels, receiving blankets—the list went on and on.

As I was dressing our new baby to leave the hospital, the pediatrician came in for a last checkup. She asked if I had everything ready at home. But when I showed her my list, she said something I will never forget: "All she needs is warmth." What I didn't know was whether I could give her enough of it.

I quickly found that the biggest obstacle to that warmth wasn't time or money, it was my selfishness. There is nothing better than a new baby to show us just how self-centered we are. I know how many times I've rolled over when my children woke up at night, or made them wait just because I was doing something for myself. To a greater or lesser degree, we all live for ourselves. Love, however, calls us to live for others and teaches us how. The warmth our children need comes from a love that asks us not only to put our wants on the back burner, but to take them entirely off the stove.

Children bring about a great change in our lives. After kids, we no longer eat the same, sleep the same, do the same things, or even like the same things we did B.C.—"before children." It's not that we suddenly fall in love with overgrown canaries or purple dinosaurs, but in loving our children, we direct more of our lives toward them and less toward ourselves. We begin to move beyond ourselves from selfishness to love.

When love conquers selfishness, it propels us in directions we would not otherwise choose. Certainly, nobody wants to change diapers or get up for a night feeding. Nevertheless, we do these things for our children because we love them. We may not like sports much, or opera either. But if we have a child with a great pitch or perfect pitch, chances are nothing will keep us out of the ballpark or the theater. Indeed, most of us love our children more than life itself. We do everything in our power to fill all their needs and many of their desires. We cover them with all the warmth and affection we can muster.

But no matter how much we love our children, we cannot be there for them all the time, and we cannot give them everything they want or need. None of us is able to protect our children from the consequences of their own choices or from the choices others around them make. The world can be an icy cold place. At times, the warmth we can give them is as insufficient as an umbrella in a hurricane.

Deep inside we all know that our love alone is simply not enough. There will always be a gap between the love each of us needs and what we can receive, even from the most loving of parents, spouses, or children. This "love gap" exists for every man, woman, and child. It is rooted in the love-hunger of our souls, which far surpasses what any human being could give us. Try as we may to fill the gap, we cannot succeed in doing so.

The fact is that although parents stand in the place of God, none of us is God. Our shortcomings, however, don't just amount to our inability to perform miracles or command the wind and the waves. What makes us deficient is not our inability to do what God does, but to love as God loves.

Throughout the life of Jesus, Mary's love for him was clear. She attended to his needs. She supported him in ministry. She never abandoned him, even when nearly all his disciples did. Though powerless, she stood lovingly beneath the cross.

While Mary gave everything she was to her Son, she did not make the mistake of thinking that her love would be enough. She knew her human limitations—that she alone was insufficient. She knew, too, that without anything or anyone else, God alone would suffice. Mary had experienced the Lord as all-seeing, all-knowing, and all-powerful. And more than that, she had come to understand that God's knowledge and power did not reside in mind or might, but in perfect love.

However much we love our children, God loves them—and us—even more. This was Mary's source of peace as she set about raising her Son. There would be and were gaps in her motherly love for Jesus, but God would fill them, just as he had for her—not sparingly, but to overflowing.

It is humbling to realize that as much as our children need us, they need God even more. As our children grow into adulthood, in some sense, they need us less and less. But as they assume the responsibilities and challenges of adult life, they will need God more and more. Without us, our children would die. But without God, they would never truly live.

The weakness of human love will fail us. Yet it is comforting to know that divine love never fails. Instead of scorning our weaknesses, God chooses to perfect his strength in them. Rather than giving us just enough of his love to get by meagerly, God floods our souls with divine passion. God loves us without limits of any kind. God never ceases to love, for love is not merely an occupation; it is the Lord's identity—for "God is love" (1 Jn 4:8).

When we come to grips with our many failures to love, whether they are frailties or infidelities, we need only turn to the love who lives in our hearts. Instead of struggling to love on our own power, we can allow ourselves to be overpowered by the love of the Holy Trinity. We must learn to fan the fires of the divine passion that burn for us and in us. And we must teach our children by example to turn to God.

God has not left us without the means to secure for our children all the love they need. Knowing the depth of human love, our Lord has provided us all with an even deeper well from which to draw. It is possible to ensure that our children will receive all the love they need for the rest of our lives. But to do so, we must give them more than just ourselves. We must give them Christ. All the canyons of our inadequacies can be bridged by the grace that flows from his outstretched arms.

O God, by the power of your perfect love, you called each of us into existence. You created us to walk in love with one another and with you. You shaped our souls to be the channels through which your love would flood the world.

Yet sometimes, Lord, I dam up your love with selfishness so that only a few drops can be squeezed from my heart. In truth I don't love anyone as much as I love myself. It is a struggle to love beyond my own borders.

Lord, I have believed and I have worked, teach me now to love. Help me to give myself to you and to others. Lord, move my heart from self-absorption to love, and live in my soul who are love itself. Amen.

Chapter 30

What's For Supper?

Breast or bottle

"Feed my sheep."

John 21:17

When we are pregnant, we don't have to think about very much. (That's probably a good thing!) Everything is on autopilot. Our unborn children eat, sleep, and "breathe" without us doing anything at all. They move and grow and develop with a level of cooperation from us that essentially amounts to showing up. Birth changes all of that. When pregnancy ends, our work begins.

So much of pregnancy is focused on birth that it can be easy to delay making the most important decisions about caring for our babies after they are born. We think about our favorite names, baby furniture, clothes, and equipment of every kind. But the first choice we really have to make for our children isn't even what to call them—it's what to feed them.

I chose to nurse our first three children and our last. I bottle-fed the others from birth. The choice between breast and bottle-feeding is a personal one in many ways, and there are plenty of good reasons to choose either.

The day I came home from the hospital with our first baby was the day my milk "came in." I was in so much pain as I walked through our apartment door that I almost quit right then and there. It took about ten days for things to calm down and settle in. But when they did, I found nursing to be a wonderful time of special intimacy between my daughter and me. Granted, it was strange to see milk squirting to the opposite shower wall. And the need to find private places often meant that I had to nurse in ladies' restrooms, dressing rooms, confessionals, and my car. I was embarrassed on numerous occasions by leaking through the thickest nursing pads simply because someone else's baby cried or I thought for a moment about feeding my daughter. But breast-feeding worked very smoothly for both of us. I really had no problems with it; and she packed on weight so fast that our pediatrician actually told me that I would probably be able to nurse twins.

I figured that nursing would be the way to go for any other children I would have. Unfortunately, it didn't work out very well for our second or third children. Our second daughter simply refused the breast when she was about a month old. Frazzled and exhausted in the middle of the night, I gave her a bottle of formula that I had taken home from the hospital. She immediately consumed it, regained her pretty pink coloring, and drifted happily off to sleep. The next day she turned purple with angry crying when I tried to nurse her. She was a bottle baby. Our son loved to nurse, but had a talent for projecting his meals across the room on a daily basis. When he was three months old, I woke up to the notion that perhaps formula would be a better choice for him. It was.

With three other children, school schedules, and the need for a little more freedom, I decided that I would not breast-feed our fourth child at all. I just couldn't imagine having the time it took to breast-feed at that point in our lives. I didn't like the idea of pumping either. The bottle was a vote for sanity and sociability. It sure looked a lot better than stress and isolation.

Bottle-feeding worked well for our whole family. I really tried to keep myself as the main connection with food, especially in the early months. But formula had the distinct advantage of making it possible for other people to help with feedings. That was something new—something I appreciated almost as much as our older kids did. In retrospect, I think that bottle-feeding contributed to my ability to "feed" both our babies and our older children in other ways. Because I did not have to be the sole source of infant food, I was more available to address all our children's need for my continued involvement in their lives. I was better able to nourish their emotional and spiritual hungers.

Whether we choose breast or bottle, the point of both methods is the same: feeding our babies. There are advantages and drawbacks to every choice we make in life. This one is no exception. Either way, feeding our babies should not provide the venue for excursions into the dark recesses of maternal guilt. I have to admit that I have never felt more guilty than when I have decided to wean a child, or not to breast-fed him at all. At some level, I suppose I believed that I was depriving our baby of something I had given our older children. But underneath it, I knew that equating good mothering with breast-feeding was ridiculous. A calm and responsive mother who bottle-fed was definitely preferable to a frazzled and exhausted mother who nursed.

My guilt in some of those instances has been so predictable and intense that I am completely convinced there has to be a chemical or hormonal basis for it. After two or three days, however, the cloud lifts, and life goes on. I was able to deal with maternal guilt by recognizing that at least part of it was rather irrational. As long as my child ate and thrived, I had no real *reason* for guilt. If we feed our children, and they eat and grow, everything is fine.

Mary didn't have a choice about whether to nurse Jesus or not. He was hungry and she fed him. But in many ways, she did have the same ongoing and daily choice we all have to feed and nurture our children, or not. Every day, our children need to be nourished. The needs they have as infants change as they grow older. But every child—every person—at every age has needs that must be met. Our earliest experiences of love are in fact exactly that: a need expressed and then filled. This is how we learn the trust necessary for intimacy.

Exotic spices and gourmet recipes are not necessary to give our children what they need. What we must do, however, is fill not only their little stomachs with food that will nourish their bodies, but we also need to find ways of filling their hearts with the love that will develop them as persons. We must learn to feed our children spiritually with ourselves. That is what Mary did, not only during her pregnancy, but long after it. Mary nourished and nurtured Jesus with all she was. Her life was his banquet table.

At the very deepest levels of our beings, we are all hungry. We fill ourselves with many things—some of which nourish and satisfy, and others which do not. None of us can eat once and be done with it. Every day brings new needs, and the same old growling stomach of the soul. Ultimately, we hunger for God. Only God can feed all we are with all of who God is. It is wonderful to realize that the infant Jesus nursing at Mary's breast would someday grow up to feed a crowd of five thousand with a few loaves and fish. That Jesus, who is the Bread of Life, shows us how to do both. While we all need to be fed, we are all called to feed one another.

O Lord, you feed me before I even know that I am hungry. You fill my every need. You nourish and sustain me with the love that you are.

Still, Lord, for me you are an acquired taste. You aren't what I think I am looking for, or what I think will satisfy me. You offer me yourself, and I search out other delicacies—sweetness that fills my mouth, but not my heart.

Help me to taste your goodness in my soul. Teach me to come to you when I am hungry. Rain down your presence upon my spirit like bread from heaven. Show me how to feed others with what you have given me, and welcome them to your table in my life. Amen.

Chapter 31

Labor and Delivery

Birthing Christ in and through our lives

> "When a woman is in labor, she has pain, because her hour has come. But when her child is born, she no longer remembers the anguish because of the joy of having brought a human being into the world."
>
> John 16:21

The purpose of pregnancy is birth. But whenever I found myself pregnant, my first thought was that I didn't want to go through labor. Like everyone else, I took the Lamaze class the first time through. When my turn came, however, I discovered there isn't much that anyone can do to prepare for childbirth.

There is a certain charm to the naiveté we all have about labor and delivery before we've been there ourselves. My own blissful ignorance was captured on film. The first photograph in our oldest daughter's baby album is one of me standing at the door of our apartment with suitcase in hand. My hair is in place, my makeup is done, and I'm smiling broadly. It was taken just before I left for the hospital.

Needless to say, that smile didn't last any longer than the hair and makeup. My innocence regarding birth fell rather quickly to the wayside. But when I happen across that photo now, I can't help but think of it as the last glimpse of the much younger, very inexperienced me. I smile to think of how I was then—and cry a little too.

The reality of childbirth is a far cry from what most of us imagine it to be. As a child, I remember thinking that a dotted line would appear on a woman's belly, and a trap door would open to let the baby out. I have to admit that some of my "adult" ideas weren't much more accurate.

My husband had his own set of misconceptions. To me, it seemed as though he was trying out for Lamaze labor coach of the year. He was ready to assume ice-chip and breathing patrol from the moment we were wheeled into the labor room. After a few hours of "pant-pant-blow," he became so annoying that I actually punched him in the stomach! In the six births that followed, my husband learned to stay in the corner and keep his head low.

In addition to our own notions, there are all kinds of wisdom regarding childbirth to be found. Historically, "feminine folklore" offered advice which is sometimes rather bizarre. My grandmother, for example, heard that if you fell asleep during labor, you were condemned to walk around with your eyes half-closed for the rest of your life. The attending nurse during her first birth must have thought my grandmother was crazy when she asked if it was all right to sleep through labor.

Today such a tale meets with immediate laughter. In our modern sophistication we have traded such mythology for a much more scientific and technical approach to birth. From my perspective, however, a thorough knowledge of centimeters doesn't do any more for a woman in delivery than did the old rumors.

There's no getting around the fact that having a baby hurts. Whether you have an "easy" birth or a difficult one, the pain of labor and delivery puts us all at the very edge of existence. Like no other experience, childbirth unites our physical, emotional, and spiritual selves at the limits of who and what we are. The intensity of sense and emotion, and the enormous significance of the birth event combine to both focus and overwhelm us. Once labor has begun, there's no turning back. We're in for the duration. All at once we are the happiest and the most miserable we have ever been.

My first three deliveries were without anesthesia. At that time, the fashion (believe it or not there are fashions!) was "natural childbirth." When it came to our fourth round, I decided to take advantage of modern medicine. Unfortunately, the anesthesia only worked on my left side. I gave birth with the anesthesiologist standing next to my bed apologizing. The last three births, though, were virtually pain free. I was actually present for a change, rather then isolated from what was happening by a wall of pain.

Although we all gather as much support and encouragement as we can, when the time comes, only a mother can birth her child. Each of us is, in a real sense, alone. Nurses, doctors, fathers, and even older children may all be in attendance. But none of them can do much more than wait and watch. As my great-grandmother used to say: "The Queen of England has servants to do everything for her. But when it comes to having a baby, even she has to do it herself."

Mary, too, did it herself. Young and inexperienced, without her mother and far from home, Mary brought Jesus into the world. There were neither classes to prepare her nor medical explanations for her to hear. All she had at her disposal was her inner strength. If anyone deserved a birthing room equipped with whirlpool, television, matching upholstery, and the best medical care, it was Mary. But for her and the Son of God, a dark and dirty stable sufficed. There was no anesthesiologist standing by. Her love for God and his Son was what she had to draw on.

Romanticized Christmas images aside, the birth of Christ is an accurate portrait of the new birth God offers to each of us. Like all babies, his birth was accomplished by suffering and hard work, and accompanied by water and blood. Eternal life is much the same.

Salvation was birthed in the pain of the cross. When Jesus' side was pierced by a lance, water and blood flowed out. We come to that moment of new birth ourselves in the sacramental waters of baptism and the eucharistic blood of Christ.

We all know that it is impossible to give birth without labor. Yet, when it comes to birthing the new life of the Spirit, we have come to expect something else—something that demands relatively little of us. At times, we may shrink from the hard work of faith. Some of us struggle to stay "pregnant," rather than go through what it takes to give birth to a new life of the soul. All of us resist the pain and anguish that often attends spiritual growth.

Just as pregnancy is for the purpose of birthing a child, faith is for the purpose of "birthing" Christ. No one would become pregnant as an end in itself. Yet it is easy to view faith in that very way. What we need to realize is that Mary's call to bring forth Christ—while unique—is not unlike our own call. Jesus first lived in Mary's womb so that he could enter the world through her. Likewise, he dwells in our hearts by grace so that he might continually enter the world through us.

Filled with the Spirit, our souls are nurtured; they grow and wait. Finally, the tiny seed of divine presence that once began silent and unnoticed in us grows beyond our ability to contain it any longer. The Christ within us becomes strong enough to be exposed to the world. In that hour called the fullness of time, we bring him forth, through our hearts and into the world. Our lives become the birthplace of Christ.

The pain of growing in faith is the pain of birth. If we suffer greatly to deliver a child, we cannot expect not to suffer in birthing Christ. Our hearts, after all, are no larger than our wombs. But despite the long weeks of pregnancy, and the pain of labor and delivery, no one doubts whether a child is worth it. Similarly, no disciple of Jesus, even the martyrs, would regret or rethink their willingness to accept the cross. The joy of his intimate presence dwarfs any hardship suffered to attain it.

How simple it is, Lord, to embark on the journey, to begin the struggle, to enter the fray. But how difficult it can be to finish the race, to complete the task, to endure till the end. The fantasies are quickly and easily embraced, but reality can be heavy and hard to bear.

Sometimes, Lord, I am so overwhelmed by my own pain that I forget what you suffered. I resist any growth that hurts. I shrink from the pangs that bring you forth. I want the blessings, but not the labor.

Lord, help me to love even when it hurts. Teach me to be sensitive to the pain others carry. Help me to follow you even when it is difficult. In the struggle be my companion, and beyond it be my joy. Lead my heart to the fullness of time. And when my hour comes, Lord, burst forth from my soul with new life. Amen.

Chapter 32

Magnificat

Gratitude as our spiritual afterbirth

Such knowledge is too wonderful for me...
Psalm 139:6

Although each pregnancy and delivery is unique, for me the final chapter of birth has always been the same. Tired as I was after the ordeal of giving birth, I could never seem to settle down and rest. With each new baby's arrival, I spent the night following labor simply too excited to fall asleep. Invariably, I've found myself during those wee morning hours thanking God for the miracle of new life.

A new baby makes our whole family more aware of how much there is to be grateful for. Tiny fingers and toes rekindle our wonder at life, and renew our sense of its frailty. The birth experience invites us all to be thankful for one another. Our children have actually thanked me for having their younger brothers and sisters.

Pregnancy and birth is mysterious and marvelous. Indeed, the whole process from start to finish is nothing less than miraculous. When we first receive those tiny babies into our arms, it's hard to fathom that we had anything at all to do with bringing them into the world. To think that just moments before, the little one we hold lived inside us. It is beyond the grasp of our understanding. It just doesn't seem possible—let alone real.

To me it seems strange that such a wonderful thing is so common to our experience. Unlike the Olympics or Haley's Comet, women give birth every day. All races, all cultures, all faiths: the great variety of humanity is recreated with each new day. As different as we are from one another, and as different as the lives we live can be, childbearing is the common denominator of feminine experience. Yet, it is unique and inexpressibly awesome every time it happens.

But as wonderful as pregnancy is, the God who blesses us with pregnancy and children is even more wonderful. Our Heavenly Father is the origin of all life; and he is the ultimate destiny of all living things. The Creator not only makes all of us, but makes *each* of us. God not only gives us life, but cares for us and calls us to share the divine life. The Holy One is always with us and within us. God longs for us to live with him and in him.

In serving this wondrous God, Mary was especially blessed. It did not take a virgin birth to convince her of the power of God's love for her. She had known it before. But unlike many of us, Mary did not lose her sense of awe for God; and she did not take God for granted.

In her humility, Mary knew that she could never earn God's love, she could only accept it. That she did with distinguished grace. Throughout her life, Mary's posture toward God was one of profound gratitude. It is, I think, the most attractive and compelling thing about her. In gentleness, Mary lived her whole life in thanks to God.

In the Scriptures Mary's words are few, but knowing her spirit it is not surprising to find that the longest passage attributed to Mary is her beautiful prayer of gratitude, the *Magnificat.* Like Mary's life, her words are wholly directed to God. In exuberant joy she speaks of her blessedness—not because of anything she had done, but because God had "looked with favor on [her lowliness]" (cf. Lk 1:48).

Interestingly, this prayer was not offered in private. While the annunciation occurred in secret, the gratitude she voiced in the *Magnificat* was a public act of worship. Mary's words recall God's faithfulness and love. Proclaiming it aloud, she shares the coming of salvation in Christ Jesus with Elizabeth and with us. With the words of the *Magnificat,* Mary leads us all in giving thanks to God.

Although it's easy to recognize that God worked miracles in Mary's life, it is also easy to overlook all the great things the Almighty has done for all of us as well. God gave, is giving, and will give us life, new life, and eternal life. In return, we need to learn how to cultivate hearts that are grateful rather than grudging. Through gratitude, God's work becomes clear to us. Gratitude reveals much of what is hidden by human pretense and pride.

More than simply giving credit where it's due, gratefulness to God secures our joy in difficult times. The psalmist teaches us that "God inhabits the praises of his people." Moreover, we "enter his gates with thanksgiving, and his courts with praise" (Ps 100:4). If we want to live in the continual presence of the Lord, as Mary did, we must learn to thank and praise God. Then our souls will magnify the Lord, and then our spirits will find joy and salvation in him.

Our unborn children growing within us shape and reshape our bodies. Similarly, Christ growing in our hearts will shape and reshape our lives. He will lead us through times of anticipation and excitement, as well as through times of exasperation and waiting. He will stir in us immeasurable joy; and he will bring us to the point of complete surrender. His Spirit will grow in us until we cannot hold him any longer, until, in labor and pain, Jesus bursts forth from our hearts.

Just as our children teach us a great deal, there is much we learn through faith about God and ourselves. Such enlightenment, however, is not the object of faith. Love is. While our objectives are often clouded and mixed, God's purpose is single and clear. Everything God does originates in love, operates by love, and is directed toward love. The great gift of faith is this love, one that flows freely when we allow God to embrace us intimately. It's the Father's will that as we allow him to embrace our hearts, we will come to embrace him in return. Our God does not want to remain a stranger.

More than wisdom or understanding, there is unspeakable joy in the loving presence of God. It is from this joy that Mary prayed the *Magnificat,* and found the strength to live it completely. Most of us could spend eternity counting our blessings—perhaps that is what happens in heaven. But of all we have to be thankful for, the greatest is our God.

My whole heart sings your greatness, O Lord, and all that I am is alive with joy. For in my nothingness your love has sought me out. Your grace has overtaken me.

How can the world not envy me? For you have done what is impossible for me—what people do not even dare to dream. You stand alone in glory.

Extending your hand to all who reach for you, you uphold them with gentle strength. But the proud, you disperse. By their own hand, they fall.

You topple the powerful, but set the weak in high places. You give to the heart that hungers, but take away from the one who fills himself.

You will not abandon anyone who serves you, for you bind yourself to your own with mercy. You guard the fruit of your Word in the hearts of those who love you; in the hearts of all you have blessed. Amen.

About the Author

Jaymie Stuart Wolfe became a Catholic in 1983 and now uses every available means to communicate the gospel of Jesus Christ. She is a frequent guest speaker for church groups and also writes a biweekly column for Boston's Catholic newspaper, *The Pilot.* Under her Loaves and Fishes Ministry, Jaymie performs concerts of inspirational music and reflection, and has produced seven recordings of original music. In addition, Jaymie and has been a regular guest of Fr. Tom Dilorenzo's *In Season and Out of Season* radio broadcast since 1990. Her first book, *The Wonder Within,* was published by Ave Maria Press in 1995. Jaymie is also a co-founder of Live Jesus, an ecclesial movement seeking to apply the spirituality of St. Francis de Sales.

A graduate of Harvard University, Jaymie is the mother of nine children and lives with her family in Wakefield, Massachusetts. Jaymie is currently pursuing a Master of Arts in Ministry at St. John's Seminary in Boston.

The Daughters of St. Paul operate book and media centers at the following addresses. Visit, call or write the one nearest you today, or find us on the World Wide Web, www.pauline.org

CALIFORNIA

3908 Sepulveda Blvd, Culver City, CA 90230 310-397-8676

5945 Balboa Avenue, San Diego, CA 92111 858-565-9181

46 Geary Street, San Francisco, CA 94108 415-781-5180

FLORIDA

145 SW 107th Avenue, Miami, FL 33174 305-559-6715

HAWAII

1143 Bishop Street, Honolulu, HI 96813 808-521-2731
Neighbor Islands call: 800-259-8463

ILLINOIS

172 North Michigan Avenue, Chicago, IL 60601 312-346-4228

LOUISIANA

4403 Veterans Memorial Blvd, Metairie, LA 70006 504-887-7631

MASSACHUSETTS

885 Providence Hwy, Dedham, MA 02026 781-326-5385

MISSOURI

9804 Watson Road, St. Louis, MO 63126 314-965-3512

NEW JERSEY

561 U.S. Route 1, Wick Plaza, Edison, NJ 08817 732-572-1200

NEW YORK

150 East 52nd Street, New York, NY 10022 212-754-1110

78 Fort Place, Staten Island, NY 10301 718-447-5071

PENNSYLVANIA

9171-A Roosevelt Blvd, Philadelphia, PA 19114 215-676-9494

SOUTH CAROLINA

243 King Street, Charleston, SC 29401 843-577-0175

TENNESSEE

4811 Poplar Avenue, Memphis, TN 38117 901-761-2987

TEXAS

114 Main Plaza, San Antonio, TX 78205 210-224-8101

VIRGINIA

1025 King Street, Alexandria, VA 22314 703-549-3806

CANADA

3022 Dufferin Street, Toronto, Ontario, Canada M6B 3T5 416-781-9131

1155 Yonge Street, Toronto, Ontario, Canada M4T 1W2 416-934-3440

¡También somos su fuente para libros, videos y música en español!